Digital Photography

Digital Photography

Mikkel Aaland with
Rudolph Burger

Random House
New York

Copyright © 1992 by Mikkel Aaland and Pond Partners

All rights reserved under International and Pan-American Copyright Conventions. Published in the United States by Random House, Inc., New York, and simultaneously in Canada by Random House of Canada Limited, Toronto.

Library of Congress Cataloging-in-Publication Data

Aaland, Mikkel, 1952–
    Digital photography / Mikkel Aaland with Rudolph Burger and Pond Partners ; Henry Horenstein, publisher, Sean Callahan, editor.
        p. cm.
    Includes bibliographical references and index.
    ISBN 0-679-74260-3 (pbk.)
    1. Photography—Digital techniques. I. Burger, Rudolph. II. Callahan, Sean. III. Pond Partners. IV. Title.
TR147.A15 1992
778.3—dc20   92-27984 CIP

Diagrams by permission of Nick Ferron

Book design by Linda Kocur

Manufactured in the United States of America

New York   Toronto   London   Sydney   Auckland

Contents

Dedication

To Ansel Adams, photographer, and Edwin Land, scientist, who worked together and who set the stage

Acknowledgments

In 1980, at his home in Carmel, California, Ansel Adams introduced me to the idea of electronic photography. With remarkable foresight and generosity he spoke of a time when his negatives — which he would donate to the Center for Creative Photography in Tucson, Arizona — would be explored using electronic scanners and computers, "allowing serious students to interpret my negatives," he said, "using state-of-the-art electronic means, in much the same spirit as a modern musician who plays Bach or Vivaldi on a modern instrument."

I'd like to thank Michael Rogers, novelist and senior writer at Newsweek, who, that same year, introduced me to the world of personal computers. His advice, encouragement, and friendship have continued to this day. Thanks to Anne M. Russell, an associate editor at *American Photographer*, who gave me my first assignment to write about the impact of computers on photography, and to Sean Callahan, the editor of *American Photographer*, who encouraged me to develop my ideas on electronic imaging.

Some years later, Sean, along with his partner Henry Horenstein of Pond Press, had the idea for this book and gave me the opportunity to write it. Sean served as the book's editor and introduced me to Dr. Rudy Burger, who would become my collaborator on it. JoEllen Bokar was of great help in reading my early manuscripts. Sarah Lazin, my agent, provided wise counsel throughout.

Kate Kelly was primarily responsible for organizing the digital gallery and contributed valuable research assistance and encouragement when it was most needed. Michael Mellin, Mia McCroskey, Laurie Calkhoven, Walt Garnett, and Ellen Lichtenstein of Random House were very supportive and helpful with their suggestions and additions.

John Harcourt of Nikon Electronic Imaging and Fred Shippey of Eastman Kodak both served as valued advisors and generously shared their time and expertise.

I'd also like to thank Paul Saffo of the Institute of the Future; Jacques Gauchey; Eric Hannah, Rachel Bernstein, and Sarah Molyneux of Savitar; Rob Fulop, Ernst Adams, and Michael Becker of Interactive Productions; Charles Wehrenberg; Sally Larsen; Ctein; John Hornstein and Anita Malnig of *MacWeek*; Alexis Gerard of Future Images; Fred Richin; Rand Wetherwax; and Seijiro Tomita, Blair D'Amico, Serge Calico, Tim Justice, Corey Halsch and Frank Logan of Sony Corporation of America.

Thanks to Henry Scanlon, Cathy Mullen, and Tom Grill of Comstock; Pam Herber of Optical Data; Bev Berg; Patricia Elste; Jan Malmestrom; Paul Drexler; Doug Rea; Wendy Vetter; Yasuo Uchida of Konica Corporation; Rick Warner of Canon Corporation; Laura Parker; Matt Herron; Philip Hopbell; Charlie Rubin; Bernard Ohaninan; Daniel Ben Horin; Steve Beck; Michael Gosney; Laena Wiltberger, Joel Hagen; Greta Mitchell; Marnie Gillette; Mike Mandel; Michelle Hammond; David Husom; Rita Dewitt; Nancy Madlin; David Shaw; Nicholas Callaway; George Wedding; Nathan Benn; Elaine O'Neill; Kim Komenich; Dan Springston; Charles Roitz; Esther Parada; Susan Felter; Brian Taylor; Carol Flax; Daryl Figueroa; Craig Hickman; Vicki Demetre; Nancy Skolos and Tom Wedell; Bruce Ashley; Michael Johnson; Sheila Pinkel; Terry Gips; Russell Brown and Steve Gutman of Adobe; Sam Merrell; and the photographers who generously submitted their work for inclusion in this book.

Finally, writing this book would not have been possible without the help of the aforementioned Rudy Burger. A brilliant engineer, entrepreneur and a true friend, Rudy gave me valuable insight and advice throughout and wrote the chapters on image transmission, output and prepress technology.

MIKKEL AALAND
San Francisco, 1992

Foreword

One of the most exciting and rewarding experiences for an engineer is to form a close working relationship with the individuals who are using the products that the engineer is helping to develop. It's been especially enjoyable working with photographer Mikkel Aaland on *Digital Photography*. His enthusiasm for this subject is apparent and I share his hope that this book will demystify the technology of digital image processing, enabling other photographers to use these new tools to create powerful and compelling images.

As off-putting as this new technology may appear to be, I believe that photographers will soon be taking this technology for granted in the same way that today's writers take their word processors for granted. The ability to correct out-of-focus or motion-blurred photographs, or alter an image with computerized photo-retouching tools will soon seem no more remarkable than the ability to move paragraphs around on a word processor or automatically correct spelling mistakes.

The technology underlying digital photography is complex, nonetheless. Those of us in the industry working to develop new digital photography products have needed to grapple with the complexities of personal computers, digital image processing, color science and traditional silver halide photography. Despite the complexity of this multidisciplinary field, the allure and immediacy of working with color images has attracted many of the brightest minds in the high-technology industry.

This has resulted in ferocious competition and has set a rapid pace of new product development, the ultimate beneficiary of which will be, as always, the consumer—or in this case a creative photographer.

This transformation from the research lab to the photo studio did not come easily, although it does seem, in retrospect, to have come almost overnight. In the early 1980s, digital image processing was the exclusive domain of scientists and engineers. We worked with monochrome images exclusively and were using, at first, mainframe and then minicomputers. The notion of doing serious image processing on the toy-like personal computers then appearing on the market for the small business user seemed absurd. The PC was regarded by us as a mere office appliance. There were no peripherals available to get anything out of the computer but streams of paper covered with unattractive, clunky characters that were more difficult to read than typewriter copy. The PC had little relevance to anyone who worked with images. Photographs, graphics, and color were not within the realm of possibilities in those early days.

A decade later, all this has changed. Personal computers have gained such power and speed that they can handle all but the most complex image-processing applications. Peripherals (scanners and printers) can take in and put out (i.e., input/output) "photographic quality" color images in conjunction with the personal computer. Image-processing software tools that were not available 10 years ago even to NASA scientists are now distributed as "freeware" on electronic bulletin boards for anyone with a PC and a modem. This has led to an explosion of new applications for digital imaging in science and engineering. But now this technology is available to photographers and publishers as well, who will take it to a new plane as they make digital photography part of the fabric of everyday life.

While it has been necessary for us developers of digital photography technology to be fluent in many areas, such as computers, digital image processing, color science and traditional silver halide photo chemistry, this complex technology will soon be made largely transparent to photographers, who will only have to concern themselves with taking the picture and determining what they want to do with it. Products such as Kodak's Photo CD, which allows users to transfer their snapshots to a compact disc at their regular processors for eventual display on the home TV, are indicative of the kind of seamless integration of digital imaging that is being anticipated. Digital imaging has moved from NASA's labs to the living room in 10 short years.

One media form after another is being revolutionized by computer technology. The written word went digital with the personal computer, music with the arrival of the audio compact disc. Now photography is going digital and its effect on society may be the most revolutionary of all.

RUDOLPH E. BURGER, Ph.D.
President, Savitar, Inc.
San Francisco, California

Part One

The Technology

Introduction
Digital Photography:
The Future Is Now

Not since its invention more than 150 years ago has photography faced such a radical change. Virtually overnight two pervasive technologies, represented by the computer and the camera, have merged. The results herald a photographic system no longer bound by many of the limits of film, a system where images can be "processed," transmitted and viewed nearly instantly, with little or none of the environmental hazards and waste created by the caustic chemicals used in traditional photography.

This revolution will have a profound effect on all photographers: news photographers will benefit from instant processing and transmission of their images by extended deadlines and more time in the field; studio photographers can set up instant electronic proofing systems and provide other billable services such as photo retouching and color corrections; photographers specializing in stock can now market images for the variety of new digital media which include CD-ROM; documentary and fine art photographers will be creatively challenged by interactive multimedia, an entirely new technology that electronically combines digital images with words, sounds, and graphics.

However, photographers are not the only ones who will benefit. Graphic artists can now add full-color photographs to their page layouts and create full-color separations without the need for expensive prepress services. Computer artists can combine computer graphics, which consist of synthetically made images, with digital photographs. Retouchers can easily port their expertise with pens and airbrush to the new technologies. People in the photofinishing business now have lucrative opportunities to set up service bureaus that offer high-end digital imaging equipment to individuals.

Not long ago only a few people had access to this new technology: the necessary equipment filled a large room and nearly cost the total GNP of a developing nation. Now, however, more advanced and powerful equipment has become available that fits on the desktop, and electronic photography is within both corporate and individual budgets.

The pace with which this technology continues to improve is phenomenal. Not a month goes by without the introduction of new digital imaging equipment—electronic cameras, scanners, imaging software, or output devices. However, despite the array of equipment, there are certain basic principles that apply to generation after generation of electronic imaging devices. And it is the principles of electronic imaging—such as the difference between digital and analog, the meaning of pixels, bits, and bytes, and the ins and outs of electronic sensors and digital printing—that are the primary concern of this book. Parallels are drawn between the new technologies and conventional photographic imaging whenever possible.

Electronic imaging was born of technology, and much of this book is technical. However, we explore other concerns as well. For example, one of the more basic perceptions of traditional photography is that photographs are indelibly etched in silver salts, and therefore don't lie. In the digital world, photographs become as fluid as a kinetic sculpture, able to be manipulated or changed with no clue left as to the origin of the work. In response to this new photographic reality, we've included important discussions on issues such as image integrity, intellectual rights, and ethics. (We've also presented examples of these "kinetic sculptures" from photographers who have explored and pushed the new technology with stunning results.)

In any case, it is our hope that *Digital Photography* will not only help creative image makers grasp a new technology as revolutionary as it is complicated, but also enable them to make photographic expressions for their own amusement, for the enjoyment of others, or for professional gain.

1.

Before You Begin

As every photographer knows, traditional photography is largely a chemical process: Silver halide crystals are oxidized when struck by light and transformed into new molecules that make up an image. With digital photography, however, much of the process is electronic, employing principles of physics rather than of chemistry.

New tools are required for electronic imaging: tools such as electronic cameras or scanners to capture or convert images into an electronic form; computers combined with image processing software to enhance or manipulate images; and devices that turn the electronic information back into something tangible, like a slide or a print or a monitor screen image. At this time there is no single, easy "turnkey" system that integrates the input of images, the processing of them in a computer and the output of the processed image into tangible form. In the future this process will change much as traditional photography itself evolved from glass plates and wooden boxes to point-and-shoot cameras with high-speed film.

Choosing the proper electronic imaging equipment—to buy, to lease, or just to borrow for experimenting—is then a most difficult task. Just wanting the best is rarely a valid criterion. The "best" in electronic imaging is often beyond the economic means of most individuals and even most small businesses. Even when access to the most powerful and sophisticated equipment is possible, there are times when it is inappropriate and unnecessary.

In the following chapters the range of electronic imaging components is discussed, from powerful to adequate, from expensive to reasonable. As readers weave their way through this material, it is helpful to keep in mind a very important question: What is the intended use? The answer to this question will invariably determine the price and power of the necessary equipment.

If one is interested in using a digital photographic system merely as sort of a scratch pad to work out ideas that will later be shot on film, then the choices of equipment are numerous and the cost of entry can be quite low (under $2,000). To achieve newspaper or magazine reproduction quality is another step up in sophistication, one that requires equipment that matches the production standards of traditional print media (and approaches the $10,000 range).

Matching the quality of 35mm film in electronic media is a bigger step yet and requires some of the most powerful imaging components made. To meet these high standards one must be prepared to pay upwards of $20,000. To set up a service bureau (i.e., the equivalent of a full-service professional photo laboratory) complete with high-end scanners, computers, and digital printers, means purchasing elaborate equipment that costs well over six figures, well beyond the means of most individuals.

New concepts also need to be learned by the photographer entering the world of electronic photography. In subsequent chapters we will describe most of them. There is, however, one very important concept—the difference between analog and digital—that needs to be explained here, in the beginning. Electronic photography is accomplished with one method or another, or a combination of both in the same system. Moving through these worlds requires knowing not only where you are, but what you are, i.e., are your images electronic signals or digital binary code?

Digital vs. Analog

Our perception of the world around us is defined by waves of energy. A sunset, a baby crying, a breeze blowing are represented by waves of light, sound, and heat. Most electronic images with which people are familiar—from broadcast TV or a VCR—are electronic signal waves. Still video cameras—relatively new electronic cameras that use CCDs (charge-coupled devices) to measure and record light energy—also store their electronic signals in continuously variable waves. The older generation of computers represented the world in terms of waves as well. They were called "analog" computers because the continuous electronic signals that they processed were analogies for their informational contents, a relatively seamless representation of measurements of sights and sounds along a continuum.

In the digital world, however, there exist only two possible discrete states, which may be expressed as on and off, open and closed, high and low. In computer terminology these states are called bits, or binary digits. (There are exceptions, where three or more states are desirable, but this is not relevant to our discussion.) What states they represent is not as important as the fact that there are only two positions in the system and one is in opposition to the other.

A binary system works in much the same way as the decimal number system, except instead of having ten digits (0–9) it has only two digits, 0 and 1. In the decimal system, nine is the last digit. To make a higher number than 9, two digits must be combined, for example 10 combines 1 and 0.

The binary system starts with 0 and ends with 1. The number "2," then, is represented by 1 plus 0 and is described as 10 (but this is not to be confused with "10" in the decimal system). The number "3" is 11 in binary. To represent "4," another column to the left must be added, making it 100. Binary numbers are too long and unwieldy for humans, but for machines, which can process millions of calculations per second, they are ideal. Every string of numbers that makes up the software code that performs a function in a digital computer consists of combinations of ones and zeros.

To create a digital photograph, an analog image is broken into a grid of pixels or picture elements, and each pixel is assigned a number indicating its location and its brightness. For color images, each pixel is assigned three numbers, one for the brightness value of each of the three primary colors. Using mathematical formulas (algorithms) the computer manipulates these points. Until a digital photograph is converted back to the analog world, it exists as an abstraction in the mathematical world, one in which you can't see or touch the picture, except when it is displayed on a computer monitor.

Besides the ease with which digital images can be processed, there are other advantages to the digital world. One attribute is that, unlike analog images, images in digital form can be transmitted or copied with no loss of quality. Duplicating the numbers in the digital file exactly produces a clone of the file. For example, repeatedly writing the equation $2 \times 2 = 4$ doesn't diminish the value of the numbers or the result. To understand why an analog image doesn't share this characteristic, think of the waves created when a rock is tossed into the water. The waves gradually diminish as they move away from the point of impact. An analog electronic image is a much more fluid and complicated structure, but it too suffers from degradation over time. As with photographic film, when duplicated, extraneous elements creep into the duplicate and degrade it. In slide duping, you gain contrast, for example. In analog signal replication you pick up an equivalent that electrical engineers call "noise."

Because all information that is processed by a computer—be it text, sound or graphics—is in digital format, digital images can be easily combined with other digitized information. This has important implications for both electronic and traditional publishing, as we will soon see.

The disadvantages of working in a totally digital environment are primarily related to cost. Digital photographs are extremely complex and cumbersome sets of digits (or bytes) that take up large amounts of storage space, be it on the computer's hard disk, or on a tape or a CD (which

---

Pixels

The basic unit of a digital image is a called a pixel. Technically, it is a mathematical equation that fixes the location of the unit in a space determined by x,y coordinates, much like latitude and longitude lines fix locations on the earth. By definition, an analog image contains an infinite number of pixels, but the actual number is limited by the various components of an imaging system: the capacity of the input device sensor (digital camera or scanner), the limitations of a screen display, and the limitations of the computer's processing ability and its software. In a sense, pixels are the building blocks of an image, not unlike the grains of silver on traditional film.

are alternate storage media for electronic images). At this time the devices required to store such data are expensive. Also, to process such huge amounts of information—even using advanced compression techniques—requires a lot of computing power, i.e., a more sophisticated computer, another ingredient that drives up the cost.

Significant Events in the History of Electronic Imaging

The history of electronic imaging—short as it is—is primarily one of a succession of related technological innovations. In the early 1920s, digital photographs were regularly sent between London and New York using a Bartlane cable picture transmission system. This system employed some very basic ideas of converting image data into numbers but the picture quality was extremely crude and the transmission took three hours. It wasn't until well after the invention of the electronic computer (1945) that electronic image processing—the alteration and analysis of pictorial information—became a practical science.

In 1957 a scientist at the National Bureau of Standards, Russell A. Kirsch, scanned the first photograph into a computer. It was an image of his baby son that marked the first time a computer could see the visual world as well as process it. Before that, computers were used primarily to process arithmetic and mathematical equations, storing that information on perforated cards. The idea of linking a monitor to a computer—one of the most significant developments in computer graphics—didn't occur until 1955.

In spite of Kirsch's pioneering work, it is the National Aeronautics and Space Administration (NASA) space program that is credited with most of the major developments in electronic imaging. On July 28, 1964, scientists at the Jet Propulsion Lab (JPL) in Pasadena, California, received electronic signals sent from video cameras on board the *Mariner 7* spacecraft on its way to the moon. The signals were extremely weak, as the cameras and transmitters of that day were limited. As the flights became more ambitious, with spacecraft flying to Mars, Jupiter, and beyond, the cameras and image processing techniques necessarily grew more sophisticated. The first cameras used orthicon tubes as sensors, which were heavy and required considerable power. The transmission was in analog form, which created signals prone to distortion. Subsequently newer cameras were developed that used vidicom tubes, which NASA helped develop with RCA.

Eventually, spacecraft signals were sent in digital form, with much better results. In digital form there were fewer variables to be affected by the hostile conditions of outer space, although there was much more data streaming down in the form of millions of bytes of information. Sophisticated computers, combined with ingenious algorithms, were able to capture these millions of seemingly mundane bits and turn them into scientifically relevant data that, when processed into color images, the general public was able to perceive as things of awe- inspiring beauty.

Interestingly, the largest body of space photographs is not man-made but largely the product of automated eyes in the skies. The technology has moved so far, fast, and profoundly, that even the idea of what a photographer is is being seriously challenged. In *25 Years of Space Photography* (published by Baxter Art Gallery, 1985), Christopher Knight writes, "The viewfinder on a spacecraft's camera is conceptual, not visual. It's a dizzying array of mathematical calculations, worked out in advance and programmed into the robotic eye; conceptual vision lets us know just when it's time to "snap the shutter."

Here on earth, the electronic imaging technology developed by NASA and JPL eventually found its way into the medical sciences, robotics, security, seismography, microscopy and military surveillance. Imaging technology was also used to help locate the *Titanic*. The remote vehicle, *Argo*, which was towed near the bottom of the Atlantic, was equipped with video cameras. But because of poor illumination, particle backscatter, and cable noise, the signals delivered to the mother ship, *Knoor*, were severely degraded. Image processing restored the signal, produced photographs, and made the enterprise a success.

In 1979, digital imaging began to move in the direction of the general public when Scitex, an Israel-based company that originally used computer graphics for designing and printing fabrics, extended its technology into the area of publishing. The company marketed the Response 300 System, a prepress technology that not only created full-color separations, but allowed an operator to change individual details of a photograph and combine images. Much of the Scitex technology can be linked to the work in image processing done by NASA a decade earlier.

Until the 1980s, image processing was accessible only to a few. (The basic Scitex setup cost hundreds of thousands of dollars.) With the introduction of the microchip, however, a process of innovation and miniaturization in business and consumer electronics brought image processing closer to the individual user. The 1980s saw the laying of the foundations of digital imaging. Among the major developments were:

- 1981—Sony introduced the Mavica, the first consumer-level electronic camera that used a solid-state chip instead of film to record images. Although it was patterned after the 35mm SLR, few were sold. It remained largely an expensive prototype until 1988 when an improved model began finding limited acceptance among photojournalists and security and law enforcement officials.

- August, 1981—IBM Corporation's PC, which used an operating system developed by Microsoft called MS-DOS or PC-DOS, effectively launched personal computing, although companies like Apple and Tandy had begun to carve out a market in the late 1970s. The IBM PC and the models that followed it in that series were designed with what was called an open architecture, which meant that other manufacturers were able to build PCs that ran on the same operating system. This enabled the PC to proliferate because different manufacturers could make machines to appeal to many different user markets.

- 1984—Apple introduced the Macintosh, the first popular computer platform with an emphasis on graphics and a "user friendly" interface, the method by which the operator directed the computer. Macintosh was a closed architecture system by comparison, which forced all developers of software to conform to an Apple standard. While this made the Macintosh more expensive than MS-DOS machines, it also made the software easier to learn and more functional for consumers. (Typically, Mac users own and use three times as much software as DOS owners.) Its popularity started the desktop publishing industry.

- 1985—Thunderscan and MacVision, two low-cost digitizers (under $200), were introduced for the Macintosh. They allowed low-resolution photographs to be represented on the home computer.

- 1986—the TrueVision/AT&T TARGA Board was introduced. The board, when placed inside the computer and used with special imaging software, brought color imaging to the PC.

- 1987—the Macintosh II brought vivid color to the Macintosh, allowing it to process 16.7 million colors.

▪ 1988—in response to the Mac II, a host of imaging peripherals for the desktop publisher appeared, among them:

Matrix produced a slide generator, which meant that images created on the computer could be output to slides.

The first desktop slide scanner by Barneyscan transformed 35mm slide images into digital files for the computer.

A continuous-tone printer by Kodak took a digital file and made a 4×5 color print from it.

ImageStudio, the first 8-bit black-and-white image-processing software program for the Macintosh appeared, followed shortly thereafter by Digital Darkroom. PhotoMac became the first 24-bit color-image-processing software but it only required an 8-bit display card. These programs were the equivalent of an electronic darkroom where exposure, contrast, color correction and cropping were made on the digital image file. In addition, retouching functions like cut and paste between different images could also be accomplished.

HyperCard, a software program offered by Apple that allowed users to create their own programs, popularized the concept of interactive media.

A number of manufacturers introduced 24-bit color cards for the Macintosh that gave it the ability to match the range of high-end color-processing stations like the Scitex.

▪ 1989—the JPEG standard for image compression was adopted. This technology was developed because the size of typical color image files was too large for most desktop image-processing systems to handle, imposing restrictions on passing images from different devices or sending them electronically. JPEG is a method of compressing the images into smaller files for increased portability and has paved the way for digital images to enter the world of telecommunications. All manufacturers have endorsed it as a standard.

Microsoft begins working on Windows 3.0, a graphical user interface (GUI) for DOS-based computers that, in a few short years, gives these machines a boost in graphics-handling capabilities, making image manipulation on them almost as easy as on a Macintosh.

The 1980s saw major steps toward practical and affordable image systems with a range of features and capabilities for a variety of users and markets. The 1990s? We are all pioneers, writing history as we go.

2.

The Electronic Camera

In the vernacular of electronic photography, the electronic camera is considered an "input device"—images are inputted from the camera into a computer. Electronic cameras operate much like a traditional camera with a lens and a shutter; however, they employ tiny solid-state chips (CCDs or MOSs) to measure and record light via an electronic process rather than a chemical one. Because they use electronic sensors, these cameras are sometimes referred to as "chip" cameras.

Electronic cameras differ from other input devices, such as scanners and digitizers, because they directly capture an external reality rather than convert existing source material into electronic form. Since they contain fast shutters, they can also freeze action and capture the "decisive moment" much better than any other input device.

There are many benefits to using an electronic camera. Images can be created and then transmitted around the world using common telephone lines. Also, images can be viewed and evaluated instantly, thereby avoiding costly reshoots. Since the storage medium is reusable, there are considerable savings in film and processing, and there is little environmental impact from packaging or chemical contamination. It is important to note, however, that at this time, most electronic cameras can't produce images that rival the quality of film. Until the technology improves (probably in the near future) the electronic camera is best used when speed and convenience are more of an issue than resolution. If the final destination of the image is a computer monitor or television screen, where resolution is inherently limited, an electronic camera is also appropriate.

There are basically two types of electronic cameras: still video and digital. Still video cameras are more common than digital cameras, which are relatively new. There is a very basic difference between the two. Still video cameras are analog. As mentioned in Chapter 1, analog simply means that information is stored in waves, not numbers. Because of this, the analog images produced by the still video camera take up less disk storage space, and are less expensive to produce than their digital counterparts. However, still video images are limited by the current resolution standards of broadcast television.

In America and Japan, where the NTSC standard is used, the maximum number of horizontal lines is 525. (In Europe and France, where PAL and SECAM standards are followed, the maximum number of horizontal lines is 625.) To understand how limiting this standard is, we only have to know that a 35mm color negative rated at 100 ISO is capable of resolving the equivalent of roughly 3,048 TV lines.

New standards for television, however, are on the way, which could mean great improvement in the quality of still video images. For example, so-called High Definition Television (HDTV), which increases line resolution to nearly 2,000 lines, already exists. Some controversy exists about exactly what form high definition television will take—one proposal is to scrap the analog transmission standard entirely and go digital instead—but it is expected that some form of HDTV will be available in the United States by the late 1990s.

Images produced by digital cameras, on the other hand, are not limited by any television standard, just by memory storage capacity. However, because there is no universal digital standard that specifies exactly how the information is to be stored, compatibility between systems is a problem.

Still Video Cameras

The first still video camera was announced in 1981 by Sony. It was called the Mavica—which is a combination of the words **ma**gnetic, **vi**deo and **ca**mera. After the Sony announcement, other Japanese manufacturers scrambled to produce prototypes of their own. Yet, because of manufacturing problems, lack of compatibility between electronic components, and unclear marketing objectives, five years passed before actual products became a reality.

In 1984, more than 40 companies agreed on a still video standard. The standard spelled out precise technical specifications for the way that electronic signals were to be recorded, much the same as the VHS and Beta format standards created for the home VCR market. In mid-1986, Canon marketed the RC-701 and shortly after, Sony began selling the Mavica A7AF. Like the Canon RC-701, the Mavica was a single-lens camera with interchangeable lenses and was part of an entire system that included a transceiver for transmitting images across phone lines, a printer, and a recorder for playing images back on a television set. The Sony and Canon cameras were followed by still video cameras from nearly a dozen Japanese companies, such as Casio, Konica, and Fuji. In 1988, a new recording standard (called Hi-Band) was adopted.

Today, cameras are widely available in both consumer and professional versions. The professional models from Nikon, Sony, and Canon, accept interchangeable lenses and generally have more complex and precise electronics. Special backs are also available that turn professional 35mm cameras into still video cameras. For example Minolta makes

Sony was the first to introduce an electronic still video camera, the Mavica, which is available in professional as well as amateur models (above). The image resolution of amateur still video has yet to match the quality of amateur film cameras, so amateur still video images are intended for TV screen output. (Courtesy of Sony)

a still video back for the Maxxum 9000. Bronica has an electronic back for their medium-format camera. There are also electronic still video backs retrofitted for traditional view cameras, but at this time they are custom-built and not widely available.

Consumer models targeted to the amateur photographer for displaying electronic family albums on a household television screen are more common. They are conceptually similar to the point-and-shoot type of compact 35mm cameras with fixed lenses, and often cost less than $500. (Some of the photographers featured in Chapter 8, "Digital Gallery," have creatively used these cameras, in spite of their limitations.)

A still video camera is only one part of a total system, which often includes a playback unit (which acts like a VCR, sending a signal to the TV), a printer (to make hard copies), and a monitor (any TV set). Printers and transmission devices are discussed in subsequent chapters.

Still Video Camera Characteristics. Both consumer and professional model still video cameras share certain characteristics. They require an approximately 2-inch floppy disk to store images. The disk looks much like a computer floppy, spins continuously while the camera is powered on, and records 50 low-resolution "field" images or 25 high-resolution "frame" images magnetically on concentric tracks. (The ability to produce "frame" images is generally a feature of the professional still video camera.) Other types of data may also be recorded on the still video disks. For example, some cameras can record 5 to 20 seconds of sound.

Most of the units now sold follow the Hi-Band frequency standard for storing images. This standard, similar to the Super VHS video standard, was introduced in 1988 and is nearly a 25 percent improvement in horizontal sharpness over the 1984 standard. (The width of the luminance portion of the signal was extended from about 10 MHz to more than 15 MHz and the white peak frequency was moved from 7.25 MHz to 9.7 MHz. The new format also specifies about 500 lines of resolution compared to 360 lines.) Since there is a still video standard, a broad range of dedicated devices can be used interchangeably from one brand to the other.

In some ways, still video cameras operate much like traditional cameras, requiring a lens and a mechanical shutter with speeds up to 1/2,000th a second. Light metering is automatic through the lens.

They have optical viewfinders, and not the electronic ones associated with most video camcorders. Some have built-in flashes, others have sync outlets for electronic flashes. Even the most inexpensive models have rapid shooting modes, ranging from 1 to 3 frames per second. Still video cameras also have a rectangular aspect ratio of approximately 2:3, which is similar to a common 35mm camera.

Determining Still Video Camera Quality. When a photographer considers buying a traditional camera he or she looks at a variety of quantifiable characteristics, such as the reliability of the shutter, the precision of electronic metering, and the resolving power of the optics. When evaluating a still video camera, many of these same considerations apply. To these familiar criteria, however, certain electronic factors must be added.

Most manufacturers advertise the quality of their camera by stating the number of pixels discernable by the camera's built-in sensor. Exactly how these sensors work is discussed in more detail later, but simply put: the more pixels a sensor can discern, the more detail it can resolve.

Purely as a measure of quality, however, pixel counts can be misleading. In fact, most sensors built today are capable of producing higher-resolution images than the NTSC standard will effectively handle (130,000 elements per frame). The way that sensors are used is also a consideration. The Sony MVC-5000, for example, uses two sensors, each capable of discerning 380,000 pixels. One sensor senses color (chroma), and the other sharpness and brightness (luminance). This results in a sharper picture. There are other electronic factors that determine the output quality of a still video camera such as bandwidth and signal-to-noise ratio (S/N).

Bandwidth is the rate at which electronic information can be transmitted through a given communication medium. Bandwidth is measured in Hz (for hertz). A thousand cycles per second is kHz (or kilohertz) and a million cycles per second is MHz (or megahertz). When sensors and other electronic components of still video cameras are operating efficiently, the amount of information "passed" to the storage device increases. For some reason, manufacturers often neglect to include this important number on specification sheets.

If a camera is not rated in bandwidth, a simple way of determining it is to divide the rated number of lines by 80 (there are 80 lines of hor-

ANALOG IMAGE SOURCES

Video disk

Video camera

Still video camera

Videocassette recorder

DIGITAL

ANALOG IMAGE SOURCES
Images that exist as analog electronic signals can originate from video disks, video cameras, still video cameras, and movie images on a VCR. They must be processed by a frame grabber board (usually located inside the computer) which turns the images into digital data for computer processing.

DIGITAL IMAGE SOURCES
Images stored in digital form reside on CD-ROM or Photo CD discs. Conventional slide or print images become digital when scanned. Soon, still cameras will be commonly available that record images digitally. (The Dycam was the first commercially available digital camera.)

Frame-grabber board

OUTPUT SOLUTIONS

Film writer

Digital printer

Floppy disk

Removable cartridge

PHOTOGRAPHY SYSTEM

HE COMPUTER (CPU)
digital photography, the
ersonal computer (some-
nes called the Central Pro-
essing Unit, CPU) replaces
e darkroom in conventional
notography. Images are
ored on the CPU's hard
sk and displayed on the
PU's monitor. Software on
e hard disk imports the im-
ges from the various sources
nd performs the desired ma-
pulations as directed by the
notographer, who uses key-
bard commands in combi-
ation with a mouse, joystick,
graphics tablet.

STORAGE SOLUTIONS
After the images are
processed they are sent from
the computer to any number
of storage media for safe-
keeping. Small images can fit
on a floppy disk but larger,
higher-resolution color images require the capacity
that can only be found on an
external hard disk, cartridge,
optical drive, or digital audio
tape. The images can be retrieved for further processing
or for transfer to hard copy
output (printing).

OUTPUT SOLUTIONS
Processed digital images can
be converted to hard copy
via a digital printer (for
paper prints) or a film writer
(for transparencies).

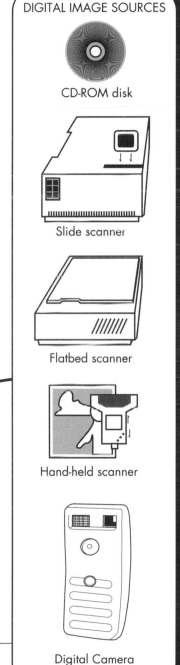

DIGITAL IMAGE SOURCES

CD-ROM disk

Slide scanner

Flatbed scanner

Hand-held scanner

Digital Camera

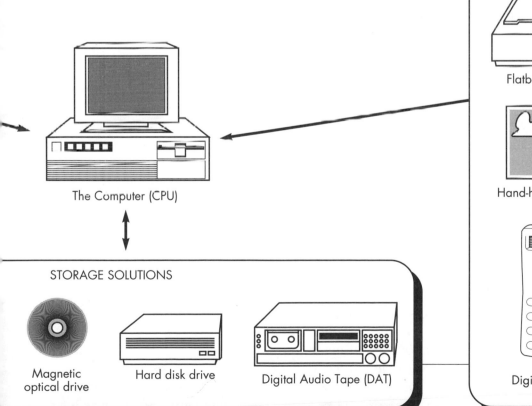

The Computer (CPU)

STORAGE SOLUTIONS

Magnetic
optical drive

Hard disk drive

Digital Audio Tape (DAT)

izontal resolution per MHz). For example, a camera rated at 500 lines of horizontal resolution (the Sony Mavica 5000) will have a 6.25 MHz bandwidth. (This is higher than the maximum NTSC level of 6 MHz.) The extra bandwidth makes little difference when a still video image is displayed on normal television, but adds quality when images are "freeze framed" by circuit boards for conversion into digital form or when still video images are printed with a digital printer.

A still video camera—like any electrical device—produces unwanted "noise." The amount of noise is determined by the quality of the sensor and other electrical parts of the camera. This noise is measured in dB, or decibels, and the relationship between wanted and unwanted noise is called signal-to-noise ratio or S/N, which can be considered the electronic equivalent of grain in film. The higher the ratio means less perceivable background "noise" and results in a "cleaner" or less "grainy" image.

There are two major components of a still video camera that generate electronic noise: the sensor/signal processor (the signal processor is also discussed in more detail later in this chapter) and the recording device. The recording device spins the 2-inch floppy disk at rates of up to 3,600 rpm. This high speed creates noise that is picked up in recording. Generally, because of the standard way in which these recording devices operate, the S/N is consistent among most cameras at 45 dB. Because S/N is much greater in other parts of the camera, the recording device is considered the weak link in the S/N of the system. The S/N of the Sony 5000, for example, separate from the recording device, is rated at 58 dB. Still video cameras rated at ratios less than 40 dB will most likely produce images with obvious snow-like effects.

Still Video Camera and Computers. Still video images must be converted into digital form before they can be manipulated on a computer. The advantages of computer compatibility are enormous. For the professional who demands control over his or her images, the ability to transfer still video images into the computer is essential. Once the image is translated into the language of the computer, software is available to enhance contrast, increase color saturation, or transform or distort it. Graphics and text can also be easily added. There are even software programs available that catalog still video images into a gallery of thumbnail-sized images, which can easily be retrieved like a data base. When a still video image is digitized, it can be transmitted around the world with little loss in quality via phone lines or satellites. (See Chapter 7, "Transmission.")

In theory, digitizing a signal from a still video camera is not a difficult task, although the early still video cameras and playback units produced non-standard electronic signals that made this difficult. There are many video digitizer boards available, for prices under $1,000, that quickly convert an analog image into digital form. (Some are listed in the glossary.) Some vendors, including Sony and Canon, bundle digitizers with some of their still video playback units. One potential problem associated with digitizing analog images, however, is color and tone calibration among camera, playback unit, and computer. There are two ways to calibrate equipment: special software (such as Savitar's Scan-Match) to match images on a computer screen to the original, or a wave form monitor—a type of oscilloscope commonly used by video engineers to display and evaluate video exposure levels.

Digital Cameras

The Dycam, the first digital camera, was introduced in 1990. Called an "image capture peripheral" by its California makers, its resolution was lower than most still video cameras and it only captured in grayscale monochrome. However, it was available for under $1,000, it stored 32 images in internal memory chips, and the resulting images could be loaded directly into a computer system without need for interim conversion.

Soon after the Dycam, Toshiba offered the Memory Card Camera, which was capable of storing twelve 400,000-pixel color images on a special memory card. It could shoot four images per second, and weighed only two pounds.

Kodak took a different approach and created special digital backs —one for color and another for monochrome only—that fit on the Nikon F-3. The resolution of the monochrome unit was rated at 1.3 million pixels. A number of other consumer electronics and photographic manufacturers are at work on their versions of a digital camera. At this time it is too early to determine the method or the timetable for the acceptance of digital cameras.

Digital cameras offer an advantage over still video cameras. While both cameras contain much of the same electronic circuitry, images in digital cameras are often stored on static "memory chips" rather than on the rotating disks of still video cameras. Thus, the digital camera is inherently less susceptible to damage or misalignment. Also, there is no degradation in a digital-to-digital transmission.

Electronic Camera Basics

Breaking Scenes Down into Pixels. Our first step is the breaking down of scenes into pixels by using tubes or solid-state sensors. Within nearly all electronic cameras, be they still video or digital cameras, is a tiny chip (no bigger than a thumbnail)—called a CCD or MOS—that senses and converts brightness values of light into electrical signals. This is the heart of the camera, and knowing the limitations of these sensors, knowing how they react to certain colors or certain light, is as essential to a photographer as knowing the characteristics of film emulsion.

In the very early days of electronic imaging, the only sensor available was a tube. Tubes, which are still used in many video cameras, are essentially vacuum glass bottles containing a layer of photoconductive material, activated by an electron beam. Tubes were (and are) extremely good for low light and high resolution, but they have inherent drawbacks: size (too big for practical hand-held cameras), memory (a contrasty moving object leaves a trail or smear), susceptibility to physical damage (glass construction), and susceptibility to light damage (they are ruined if exposed to direct sun).

In the early 1970s, scientists invented the solid-state sensor, a remarkable device that made the production of a consumer filmless camera and other industrial and military products possible. There are several types of solid-state sensors, but CCDs (charge-coupled devices) and MOS (metal-oxide semiconductor) sensors are the most common. All are tiny, measuring only a few centimeters in diameter, and wafer thin. On the minute, two-dimensional surface are tens of thousands of discrete capacitors (or diodes or conductors), which collect and determine light intensity.

Unlike tubes, solid-state sensors are less susceptible to breakage and rarely wear out. They use less power than tubes and accept large amounts of light without damage. They also don't have "memory," so the problems of motion blur are virtually nonexistent. Magnetic, radar, and microwave fields—which literally distort the electron beam of a tube sensor—will not affect the solid-state sensor.

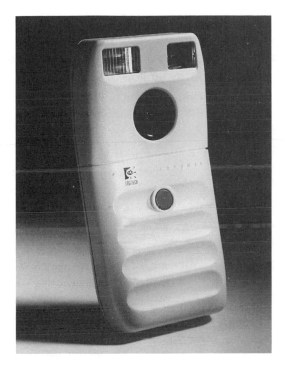

Dycam manufactures the Fotoman for Logitech. Electronic cameras are useful in situations where low-resolution output is acceptable, such as in newsletters, on ID badges, etc. The unusual design is attributed to a lack of removable recording media. Images are stored in memory and when full (after 32 images) the camera must off-load the data to an external storage medium. (Courtesy of Logitech)

On the other hand, like any new technology, solid-state sensors aren't perfect. High resolution is difficult to achieve because of inherent production problems (cramming more and more capacitors into a single chip increases the likelihood of failure). There have also been problems making the sensors more sensitive to light: most sensors only achieve an equivalent ISO of 80-150 for color and 400 for black-and-white. Solid-state sensors also tend to produce more "noise" than tubes, especially in low light situations.

In principal, tubes and solid-state sensors work in the same way. They both break a scene down into tiny components called pixels (picture elements), tubes by using grids, solid-state sensors by using discrete capacitors. Within each pixel, light values are discerned and recorded. The resolution increases as the sensor is capable of breaking the scene down into smaller and smaller pixels.

To better understand this concept, think of a hand-held light meter. Like the sensor in a filmless camera, the light meter converts photons into electrical pulses. Most light meters average the light over an entire image—and prompt a needle to move or a digital display to read. However, since the meter reads the scene in its entirety, it discerns only one giant pixel, so to speak, and no individual detail is noted. Now, if you were to focus the light meter tightly, as if it were a spot meter, and point it carefully from left to right, line by line, at hundreds or thousand of points in an image, and then record each reading, you'd have a record of what the image looked like. This is essentially what a sensor does.

The first solid-state sensors were able to resolve fewer than 100,000 pixels. Now there are sensors available that resolve up to 4 million pixels. As comparison: tubes can resolve over 3.5 million pixels and color negative film up to 15 million pixels. In contrast, the human eye can resolve up to 125 million points (or pixels) of light.

Exactly how different sensors work is complex and characteristics vary. The most commonly used tube sensor is the vidicom tube, known primarily under the trade names of Saticon, Newvicon, and Plumbicon. These tubes differ mainly in the type of photoconductive material used. They come in sizes ranging from 1/2-inch to 1 1/4-inch. The larger sizes, of course, are more expensive and able to resolve more detail.

The CCD solid-state sensor differs from the MOS sensor primarily in the way that light values are discharged by the diodes: CCDs pass the signal from one diode to the next, either vertically or horizontally, in a bucket-brigade fashion while the MOS sensor addresses each diode individually. The former results in a sensor with slower sensitivity, but yields better resolution and color.

Signal Processing. The next step—after a scene is broken into pixels and electrical pulses—is signal processing, performed by another solid-state chip residing in the camera. The signal processor completes many tasks: it converts the electrical signal into either digital or analog form, encodes color, and can even extend dynamic range. In a sense, it functions much like the human brain, which converts the stream of continuous raw data from the eye into distinct shapes and colors. The eye, with its seven million cones collecting color and 125 million rods sensing light and dark, is much like the sensors described above.

Technically a sensor does not sense color, it only perceives gradations of brightness. Color is reproduced through a process similar to the one used for color film (black-and-white silver halide layers filtered through built-in dyes). Red, green, and blue filters are incorporated into the sensor and, through signal processing, the three primary colors are mixed and other colors are created.

In the future, cameras might well be equipped with signal processors that turn a sensor into a shutter, allowing for speeds that could never be achieved mechanically, and that could even program a camera to ignore blur and camera movements.

Storage. Unlike film—which functions both as sensor and storage device—the filmless camera employs a separate means of storing information. There are various ways of doing this, depending on whether the camera saves the information in digital or analog form. A still video camera, which stores analog information, uses magnetic media, specifically a two-inch floppy disk. No agreement has been made at this time for a common digital storage standard, a situation that is likely to change, but the two digital cameras currently on the market both use solid-state RAM (random-access memory) chips to store the image information.

Electronic Camera Use

Although there are many similarities between electronic and traditional camera operations, some differences must be explained. The following applies to both still video and digital cameras.

Lighting and Exposure. When shooting with an electronic camera, all the general rules (and contradictions) of traditional lighting, composition, and tone remain. However, at this time, electronic cameras are not capable of the dynamic range of traditional film-based systems. Something that produces marginal shadow detail on film will show no detail at all with most electronic cameras. Until better sensors are developed, adjustments must be made. Lighting ratios, which for film might go as high as 8:1, must be decreased to as low as 3:1.

Electronic cameras are programmed to balance at daylight temperatures (5,900 K), the same as most film. This means that all the traditional rules of balancing and mixing color apply. Shooting tungsten lights without filter compensation will result in a reddish cast; fluorescent without correction will result in a green cast, mercury vapor lights go blue-green, while sodium vapor lights go yellow.

Color correction can be made in several ways: by filtration of the source light or the camera lens, or adjustments of the white balance setting (on professional models only). Some color correction can be made later, in a computer, using such programs as PhotoShop. (See "Off-the-shelf Software Programs" in Part Four.)

Although an image from an electronic camera can be instantly viewed on a monitor, monitors are notoriously unreliable and inaccurate. What you see on one monitor will differ from what you see on other monitors or what is produced on printing devices. Systems, therefore, should be pretested before actual use. Monitors can also invite lighting by "committees" of assistants, art directors, and clients, which is seldom desirable.

In short, remember that while there are a number of ways an image can be improved after the recording process, correct exposure is essential. There is no substitute for a properly exposed still video image. Also, the best control over color is through lighting and camera filters, or careful control of props and costumes, rather than electronically through white balance correction or post-production techniques.

Shooting. Many of the professional electronic cameras are much heavier than the typical 35mm camera. Monopods are highly recommended to minimize shutter flutter and tired arms. Because of quality limitations, cropping should be tight to avoid enlarging and the subsequent loss of image quality.

Carry spare batteries or find a power source. Electronic cameras drain much more power than conventional cameras. If using an electronic still video camera that requires disks, have plenty to spare. Although they are reusable, the disks can only be erased by a separate playback unit .

Electronic sensors are effectively one-quarter the size of a 35mm image; therefore the focal length of a lens sized for a 35mm camera must be multiplied by a factor of four for electronic cameras. A lens that is considered normal (50mm) for a 35mm camera is the equivalent of a 200mm lens, a 100mm lens becomes a 400mm lens, and so on. Considering that a 16mm lens is a "normal" lens on a still video camera, obtaining wide angle shots on a still video camera can be a problem. (A 12–72mm zoom lens on a still video camera is effectively a 48–288mm zoom on a 35mm camera.)

Avoid, if possible, shooting scenes or subjects with closely knit horizontal and vertical lines (e.g., plaid clothing or venetian blinds). Because of the nature of the sensors, this creates bleeding and noise in the final image. Spectral reflections and extreme highlights cause noise or image speckles.

The Future

At this time, there is no question that film has higher resolution, more dynamic range and is much less expensive than any electronic alternative. But film has nearly reached its theoretical limits in sharpness and sensitivity, and the electronic camera is in its infancy. If the current pace toward technological progress is continued, the electronic camera may rival and even surpass the qualities of film.

Does this mean the end of photography as we know it? Probably not. Instead, what will probably occur is a synthesis of the digital world and film. Low-cost scanners (Chapter 5) are already making it possible to get the best of both worlds by shooting in film and scanning the result for computer manipulation and transmission. The world is not shrinking. It is expanding.

3.

Computers:
The Digital Darkroom

To illustrate how a computer functions as an image processor or digital darkroom, it helps to compare it to the human brain. Basically, a computer takes in a variety of information (input), processes it, and produces a result (output). While the human brain receives information from the sensory organs, the computer receives its information from peripherals such as a digital camera, scanner, keyboard, or mouse. To create images, the brain interprets raw impulses sent from the optic nerve, changing them into discernible and familiar shapes and forms. The computer uses pulses of electrical energy to do the same. Normally, the brain operates as a very efficient image analyzer, allowing us to navigate through the physical world with ease. It takes an altered state—induced by drugs or sleepiness—for the brain to become an image enhancer. Computers must use special software—a set of mathematical instructions that tell the computer what to do—in order to process or enhance or manipulate images.

Computers come in all shapes, sizes and forms. There are computers that cost millions of dollars and are used by large military and scientific research institutions to perform incredibly complex tasks, and others that are used by large corporations for everything from tracking inventory to financial planning. These are usually mainframe computers, and they are normally accessed by many users through so-called "dumb" terminals, which are really only monitors and keyboards with little or no built-in computing capacity.

However, it is the personal computer (PC) that has the most relevance to photographers interested in electronic imaging. The PC, which made its appearance during the late 1970s, is defined as a self-contained unit consisting of a central processing unit, a monitor, and a keyboard. It is generally operated by one person at a time. It is often connected to a local area network that allows several PCs to share printers, scanners, and other devices.

Personal computers are also known for their affordability, but this is a very subjective criterion, depending on one's budget or financial resources. Some of the most powerful personal computers can cost as much as $10,000, although personal computers with enough power to do serious electronic imaging can be purchased new for prices ranging from $2,500 to $6,000.

Another category of computers with significance for photographers interested in electronic image processing is the workstation, manufactured by such companies as Sun, Silicon Graphics, and NeXT. These powerful computers—which operate faster and more efficiently than early mainframe computers—often cost $10,000 or more, which puts them beyond the means of most individuals. Like everything else in the computer industry, the price of workstations is expected to drop and may eventually approach the price of PCs. As workstations drop in price, however, PCs continue to improve, and the distinction between the two is expected to disappear.

Personal Computer Platforms

The personal computer industry is divided into so-called platforms, combinations of specific kinds of hardware and software. At this time there are basically three personal-computer platforms that offer the combination of hardware and software required in electronic imaging at a price that an individual can afford. These are the Apple Macintosh, the IBM and IBM compatibles, and the Amiga line of computers from Commodore. Within each of these platforms is a variety of models—not all of which are appropriate for image processing.

Each platform is distinct from the others; the software for one kind of hardware will not work on another. Fortunately connectivity and data transfer between the Macintosh and IBM PCs have dramatically improved in recent years. However, the different platforms can only share some information and very few peripherals, and therefore great care must be taken in choosing the right platform.

There are many factors in choosing a computer platform appropriate for electronic imaging. Purely from a technical point of view, however, a computer hardware platform should be chosen according to the availability of software. (Price, service availability and support are also important and are discussed later.) A photographer interested in image enhancement or manipulation, may, for example, be especially taken by a program that is available only for the Apple Macintosh. Or a photographer may prefer a program written for use only on the DOS platform. In some cases, software packages are available that run on several platforms making software less of a determinant. (Imaging software is the specific topic of the following chapter.)

To a lesser degree, you should also ask: What peripherals do I need and with what platform do they work best? Peripherals include such items as scanners, frame grabbers, monitors, and printers. Although peripherals are sometimes made to work on different platforms, this is not usually the case.

There are distinct differences among the three personal computer platforms—the Apple Macintosh, for example, is known for ease of use, the IBM compatibles for their expandability and lower prices, and the Commodore Amiga for its reasonable price. None of them is intrinsically better than another: they all have unique value depending on application, price range, and service availability.

IBM Compatibles (DOS and OS/2 systems). DOS—which stands for Disk Operating System—is the name of the operating system written by Microsoft for computers that are built using the standards developed by IBM. OS/2 is the newer operating system, written for IBM's most powerful personal computer line, the PS/2. IBM introduced its first personal computer in 1981 but since it was an "open" system, other vendors quickly offered clones or look-alikes. Because of the marketing clout of IBM and their success in using the strategy of an open architecture, the PC (which has gone through significant improvements) enjoys the biggest market share in the computer industry. Because of this large installed base, there is a huge number of electronic imaging hardware and software options for the PC and its clones, most of it competitively priced. DOS computers can be somewhat difficult for the uninitiated to use, however, so Microsoft created the Windows operating environment to give them a more "user friendly" look and feel. Windows is a graphical user interface (GUI) that gives program developers a standard graphical environment within which they can build their user programs. It also enables a high-resolution monitor to display a text or graphical image almost exactly as it should appear on a printer or plotter. This is the same type of environment that has been the hallmark of the Apple Macintosh.

Macintosh Computers. Apple Computer was founded in 1977 by Steve Wozniak and Steven Jobs, the renowned duo who started their company in Jobs's garage and went on to create a multibillion dollar computer giant. The Macintosh, introduced in 1984, was a "user friendly" computer, the first personal computer to present computer graphics to a wide audience. Their introduction of the LaserWriter two years later helped create what is now known as desktop publishing. The user-friendly concept was achieved by creating a generic-looking desktop environment (actually called a "desktop") with icons representing such familiar office tools as a wastebasket and file folders. Instead of typing in a command, a user could use a mouse—a puck-like device that translates hand movements to invisible x,y coordinates on the screen—to select and then execute various commands such as "open a file" or "launch an application." To achieve this easy-to-use, intuitive system, Apple chose to keep it a closed system. That meant that the major components were designed and marketed only by Apple, making the Macintosh generally more expensive than other platforms.

Commodore Amiga. The Amiga—introduced by Commodore in 1987—incorporated many of the features of the Macintosh, such as a user-friendly, icon-based, mouse interface, all for a lower price. It even employed the same microprocessor chip as the Macintosh.

The Amiga is especially popular in Europe and is used in TV stations worldwide because of its video-editing capabilities. In this country, for a variety of reasons, including poor marketing, it usually doesn't get the attention it deserves.

Not only is the Amiga a low-cost alternative to both the Apple and

DOS computers, but it potentially contains all the power and speed required for sophisticated color-image processing.

It's true that in the not-so-distant future many of the major distinctions that separate one platform from another will probably disappear: Macintoshes are already more "open," meaning that they accept peripherals from outside vendors. Cheaper DOS machines running under Windows are almost as "user friendly" as the Macintosh, and the Amiga's user base is increasing as its features become more widely known. This could leave us in a world not unlike the camera world where Nikon or Canon or Minolta products are chosen for subtle rather than intrinsic differences.

Choosing an Individual Model

Within each personal-computer platform are individual models. These models are identified with numbers and letters such as the Macintosh IIfx or the PC AT or the Amiga 1000. These names do little, however, to indicate whether a particular model is appropriate for electronic imaging. You need to examine three characteristics: operating speed, internal memory, and expandability.

Internal Operating Speed: Chips, Buses, and Clocks. The internal operating speed of a computer is determined by the type and rated speed of the microprocessor chip, the method used for transferring data to and from the chip, and the speed of the internal clock. The more quickly these components can operate, the more quickly a computer can process an image. There are other external factors, such as the speed of a hard disk and the efficiency of the software, that also have an effect on the overall performance of a system. We will discuss these external variables in other sections.

Loosely speaking, the operating speed of a particular computer model affects the creative process in much the same way that using one photographic paper or developer can produce faster, easier results than can another. However, with computers, increased speed has no effect on the quality of the ultimate print, as is sometimes the case in traditional photographic processes.

The rate at which a chip processes mathematical calculations is expressed in bits. A 16-bit chip, therefore, will process more information more quickly than an 8-bit chip. (All Macintoshes use a 32-bit chip. The first IBM PC used an 8/16-bit chip, a subsequent model—the AT—used a 16-bit chip, and the latest models use a 32-bit chip.)

It doesn't matter how quick a chip is if the path that information must take to get to it isn't big enough. These pathways are called "buses," and each computer company uses its own bus, just as it uses its own chip: Apple uses the NuBus, most DOS computers use buses called ISA for Industry Standard Architecture, the new IBM PS/2 uses a proprietary bus design called Microchannel Architecture, and the newest PC clones use a bus called EISA or Extended Industry Standard Architecture. The Macintosh NuBus is a 32-bit bus as are the IBM Microchannel and the EISA. A 32-bit bus is twice as wide as a 16-bit bus, and is able to carry streams of information much faster. The size of the bus and the size of the chip don't have to match—a 32-bit chip will work with a 16-bit bus—but it is easy to see that a fast chip won't be of much good unless it can receive and transmit information via a comparable bus and vice versa.

There is one more important factor in determining the internal processing speed of a computer: the internal clock. The clock—an oscillating piece of crystal—is the ultimate authority in the computer. By generating a signal at periodic intervals, it regulates activity, keeping everything moving properly, like a drummer or a bass player in a band. Nothing can happen without a clock pulse; if the clock missed a pulse, every circuit on the chip would be frozen for that instant.

The rate at which the clock sends out pulses is measured in megahertz. One megahertz is one million pulses per second. A clock may run at 33 megahertz, which means the microprocessor is performing up to 33 million tiny operations each second. Often one sees computers rated in MIPS or **M**illions of **I**nstructions **P**er **S**econd. This can be roughly equated to clock speed or millions of pulses per second. However, MIPS is not really a precise method of measuring computer speed because some instructions take longer than others. For example, adding might take 2 pulses to perform one instruction while division takes 50 pulses to perform one instruction. MIPS, then, is just an approximate guide to performance.

To help understand how the bus and the clock speed affect computer processing speed, think of the bus as a common water pipe, the data that it carries as water, and the clock as the water pressure. A big hose, then, with lots of pressure, pushes a lot of water (data) back and forth. A big hose with little pressure (i.e., a slow clock) dribbles water (data) back and forth. A small hose (i.e., an 8-bit bus) will take more time (i.e., many more clock pulses) than a wide hose (i.e., a 16-bit bus) to do the same operation.

When you buy a particular computer model, chips, buses, and clock speed are fixed parts of the package. There are ways to "boost" a computer's performance by using devices such as accelerator boards and digital image-processing boards. However, using these peripherals is not always desirable because of compatibility problems. It is always best, when possible, to buy the computer that comes with the fastest internal processing components as standard.

Internal Memory: RAM and ROM. Internal processing memory is divided into RAM and ROM. When choosing a particular model, it is the RAM capacity that is important.

RAM—random-access memory—is the place where the computer processes images, and temporarily stores them until a more permanent storage place is found. A typical color photograph may take up six megabytes of memory, the same memory required for 200,000 words. Because of these extensive memory requirements, RAM capacity becomes very important in dealing with images.

ROM—read-only memory—is memory that is permanently programmed inside a computer, even when the power is removed, holding part of the computer's operating system. It cannot be added to or changed during the normal operation of the computer. It is not a major factor in determining a particular computer model to be used in image processing.

RAM must have uninterrupted power—a momentary interruption and all the data is gone, never to be retrieved. The speed at which RAM operates is controlled by the internal clock, and when additional RAM chips are purchased to upgrade a computer, they must be rated to run at the required speed.

Because imaging software creates duplicates or even triplicates of an image to enable certain processing tasks, it is ideal to have enough RAM to be able to hold two or three full copies of the full digital image. A 6-megabyte image, then, would require 18 megabytes of RAM. Since this is more RAM than can currently be installed in most personal computers, a software technique called "virtual memory" is commonly employed. Virtual memory allows only part of the image to be in memory at any one time, while the rest is stored on a floppy or hard disk. The major disadvantage of virtual memory, however, is that the computer slows down as the image components are swapped back and forth between disk and RAM.

Computers come with some RAM installed, but additional RAM can be purchased. Again, the amount of RAM that can be added is limited by the particular computer model.

Expandability: Slots and Ports. Because image processing requires an array of peripherals—scanners, printers, high-resolution monitors, video digitizers, etc.—a computer must have the capacity to "expand" and connect to each component. These devices connect to the computer either through a slot that connects directly to the computer's internal bus or through a port, one of the external receptacles in a computer to which a peripheral is connected via a cable.

Slots are like an empty parking spot, placed inside a computer, waiting for special cards that expand the capacity of the computer. Typically slots are used for graphic expansion boards, which generate the analog signal necessary for a monitor, or disk drive controllers, or a digitizer, which takes in an analog signal and converts the information into digital form. Because the number of slots is often limited on most computers (eight is usually the highest number), multiple-purpose cards can also be purchased.

Macintosh and Amiga computers connect to many of their peripherals—printers, mice, modems, networking links—via specially designated ports that require no expansion cards and therefore take up no slot space. Since PCs have only a few built-in ports, some peripherals may have to be hooked up via ports built into expansion cards..

There are different types of ports/bus connections or interfaces. The type of port/bus largely determines the speed at which a computer accesses and sends information to and from a peripheral.

PC and Amiga computers primarily use serial and parallel ports for normal peripheral communication. Apple computers use a proprietary AppleTalk port for normal peripheral communication. The PC has a port dedicated solely for use by its keyboard, while the Amiga and Apple use an input port to which you can "daisy-chain" (connect from one peripheral to another in a chain) a keyboard, mouse, trackball, graphics tablet, or other input device. Amiga and Apple also use the much faster SCSI port for communicating with high-speed peripherals like hard disk drives, where the PC uses expansion cards for hard disk drives and other high-speed peripherals. High-speed image processing frequently requires even faster communication speeds, so image processing expansion boards sometimes use special GPIB or IEEE-488 interfaces which are optimized for graphics applications.

Serial ports, also called RS-232 ports, transfer data between the computer and a single peripheral rather slowly. They have a top speed of about 20,000 bits per second. Serial ports transfer their information down a single wire as single bits of electrical information, one bit at a time. They are very reliable and can be used to communicate over distances greater than 2,000 feet. They are most often used for modems, mice, plotters, and hand-held scanners—relatively slow-speed devices.

Parallel ports are somewhat faster than serial ports. They transfer data between the computer and a single peripheral over eight wires simultaneously—one byte (eight bits) at a time. They have a top speed of about 200,000 bits per second. Parallel ports are usually used to communicate with printers, plotters, slide printers, and other such output devices. Parallel port cables are limited to about 10 feet, after which they start losing data.

AppleTalk is a high-speed serial port on Apple Macintosh computers. It is used to communicate with multiple peripherals and between computers. It has a top speed of about 150,000 bits per second. Cables are daisy-chained and several peripherals can be connected on a single network. AppleTalk cables can be used to about 200 feet before signal errors start to become serious.

SCSI (Small Computer Systems Interface) is a high-speed parallel port standard used to communicate with multiple high-speed peripherals, such as hard disks, image processors, and high-resolution color scanners. SCSI ports have a top speed of about 5 megabits (million bits) per second. Cables are daisy-chained and several peripherals can be connected on a single network. SCSI port cables are limited to about eight feet, after which they start losing data.

GPIB (General Purpose Interface Bus) or IEEE-488 interfaces are highly specialized parallel ports that require an expansion card for all microcomputers. They are used only with the very highest end image capture and digitizing peripherals, or with specialized printing devices. Cables are daisy-chained and several peripherals can be connected on a single network. GPIB cables can be used to about 25 feet between peripherals before problems occur.

Purchasing a Computer

As we've already mentioned, a computer is ideally chosen on the basis of software availability, then operating speed, expandability and peripheral needs. Beyond these technical considerations purchase decisions are based on such things as price, service warranties, and support.

Price is largely a function of where you buy the equipment. Mail-order companies often offer the lowest prices, but as any photographer who has bought camera equipment this way knows, warranties and technical support may be lacking. However, some mail-order sources for computers are extremely reliable. In addition, because the personal computer industry is extremely competitive, if you walk into a retail store with a published, mail-order price in hand, shops are often willing to meet or at least come very close to the lower price.

Timing is another important factor in getting the best price. Just after the announcement of a new model, current but now "older" models are rapidly discounted to encourage sales and to make room for the new inventory. Educational discounts are another way of getting a bargain. Many computer companies sell computers to schools, colleges, and universities at a greatly reduced price. They then offer the computers to students, spouses, and family members at prices typically 40 to 60 percent off list price. User groups can also receive group discounts, which they can pass on to their membership. Note that prices for computers in the U.S. are the lowest in the world, so shopping overseas—as we used to do for camera equipment—is a big mistake.

As you wade through the mass of advertisements and conflicting prices, keep in mind that not a single computer would be sold if everyone waited for the perfect computer at the perfect price. You should assume that any computer you buy now will most likely be replaced by another in two or more years. This actually may be comforting to those who are afraid of making the leap for fear that they will make the wrong decision.

Used computer equipment should always be considered for pure value. Computers have few moving parts and rarely deteriorate. The parts that break on the computer (the power supply, the disk drive) are generally not too expensive to replace. Used equipment can be purchased through the classified sections of local newspapers, through computer "swap meets," and through the employee bulletin boards of large companies or corporations.

Although the computer itself is generally maintenance-free—especially compared to other computer-related devices such as monitors and scanners—a service warranty of at least a year is highly desirable. If something is going to go wrong with a computer, it generally happens during the first few months of use. While extended warranties should definitely be considered for peripherals that are known to malfunction—like scanners, hard drives, and printers—purchasing an extended warranty on the computer itself is not generally considered a good value.

Finally, any decision regarding computer equipment should take into consideration the availability of technical support. Unless you know how to set up and use the computer, the best bargain is worthless and the best equipment is useless. Support comes in many forms: knowledgeable friends; fellow photographers who have tested particular platforms and software; and user groups that can steer a photographer to the best bargains in town and away from unscrupulous dealers. Support can also mean hiring an independent consultant and paying anywhere from $25 to $100 an hour for services. In just a few hours a consultant can give advice that may save days of frustration or thousands of dollars in unnecessary purchases.

It is difficult to buy a computer without help. But a quick browse of the yellow pages or a call to a professional photography or computer organization or to a user group will reveal an ever-expanding network of people eager to help.

Storage Devices

Some sort of storage device or combination of devices is essential in any photographic imaging system, not only for working on the image (in conjunction with RAM via virtual memory) but for distribution and archiving of information. Many computers come with some sort of storage medium built in, but because of the memory requirements of electronic imaging a photographer should assume that he or she will need to add more.

The two major considerations for choosing storage devices are storage capacity and the speed at which the device accesses information. Access speed is less important when a device will be used primarily for archiving or storage and not as part of the working memory.

Storage capacity is rated in megabytes or gigabytes of information. As we have frequently mentioned, images take up huge amounts of space. While the average size is between 125 kilobytes and 5 megabytes, one image can be as large as 80 megabytes. This means that it is nearly impossible to have too much memory, and any storage devices that will be at all practical for electronic imaging must hold at least 80 megabytes of information.

Speed is determined by the design and type of memory device and the way in which the device is hooked up to the computer. The speed of the disk is expressed as the average length of time, usually in milliseconds, that it takes the disk drive head to move from one place to another and access information. A relatively fast hard drive might be rated at 12 milliseconds, while a slow drive (such as the original hard drive installed in the IBM XT) might be rated at 85 milliseconds. Floppy drives, the kind that usually come with the computer, are so slow they are generally not rated.

Floppy Disks. These are the most common type of storage medium and are considered a feature, rather than an option, of a desktop personal computer. They commonly come in 5¼-inch and 3½-inch formats—the former somewhat flexible and the latter in a stiffer case. Newer 2-inch disks, such as those used in some high-end "notebook" computers, are becoming available. The normal storage capacity for floppy disks is between 360 kilobytes and 1.44 megabytes, depending on size and density. They are used for the sale and transport of software programs (although many of today's programs fill several floppies) and for back-up of critical data and long-term data storage. When used with various compression techniques (discussed in Chapter 7), they can be used to transport and store images, albeit at low resolution. Special very high density 3½-inch floppies can hold as much as 20 megabytes, but these have not yet achieved widespread usage and cannot be used with most service bureaus.

Hard Drives. These contain thin platters of magnetic material, which are sealed in a clean, airtight space. These platters revolve at extremely fast speeds. Hard drives exist for virtually all computers, and since they are so prevalent, prices are quite competitive. The smallest hard drive holds 20 megabytes of information but there are hard drives that can store gigabytes of information available for certain platforms. Hard drives are delicate but can be transported. The drives with removable cartridges, discussed below, are recommended if portability will be required. What is important for image processing is the speed of the disk, and the size. The more storage capacity, the better.

Removable Storage Media. An extremely convenient form of memory storage for digital photography are the so-called bottomless drives, which use removable cartridges containing built-in hard drives or optical laser discs to store information. These drive capacities are only limited by the number of discs or cartridges one owns. Generally, for technical reasons, these storage drives access information at a slower rate than hard drives. This can become frustrating for a photographer as he or she waits for a 10-megabyte image to be served up.

Cartridge drives. There are three basic types of removable cartridge drives: the Bernoulli drive, the Syquest drive, and the Ricoh drive, all of which contain a removable cartridge capable of storing 44, 88, or 128 megabytes of information . These drives are sold by a variety of second-party vendors. Although similar in concept and design, each type of drive uses its own proprietary method of reading and writing information and therefore cartridges are not interchangeable.

Of the three, the Syquest drive is the most common—it is a standard among service bureaus where photographers go to have hard copies of their images made—and is therefore recommended. Removable cartridge hardware generally costs between $450 and $1,000, and the removable media itself between $70 and $150. Although removable drives cost more, the amount of data they store, and the endless number of cartridges that you can access, bring the cost per megabyte down to a point where they are more economical than hard drives with fixed-media discs.

Optical Memory. Optical Memory includes CD-ROM and other computer CD formats. Physically these discs are exactly the same as the common audio CDs; they are thin, shiny platters with a distinctive rainbow sheen. As with audio CDs, the information is read by a laser beam rather than a magnetic device. Indeed, most CD-ROM drives can also read and play regular audio CDs. CDs can only be written once, when they are initially "pressed" at the factory. There are CD mastering devices available, but they are very costly and are generally impractical for the average photographer.

CDs are good for transferring information and programs but not for everyday memory storage. They don't operate nearly as fast as most hard drives. But what they lose in speed and convenience they make up in storage capacity. One disc holds up to 650 megabytes of unformatted data, which is equal to 700 floppies. The drives cost from $600 to $1000, and discs filled with useful data such as dictionaries, clip art, sound, fonts, games, and even digitized stock photographs can be bought for as low as $50.

Magneto Optical Devices. Magneto optical devices use CD laser technology, combined with magnetic technology, to both read and write information to disc. They are expensive, costing $3,000 to $4,000, and extremely slow, but offer the same huge capacity as other CDs. They have the added convenience of enabling you to add and remove (erase) images.

Digital Audio Tapes (DAT). DAT tapes not only store music but when used with a special DAT drive, can store computer data as well. Considering that a DAT tape typically costs around $10 and will hold two gigabytes of information, they are by far one of the cheapest ways of storing information. However, their access time is so slow that they are used practically only for backup and long-term archiving of images. VCR tapes, which hold up to 10 gigabytes of information, are another economical, albeit slow, way of storing information.

The Future

No longer are computers the complex and expensive tools of a privileged few. As they become even more inexpensive and powerful, the majority of professional photographers will employ their electronic image-processing capabilities in some way.

The confusion that is created because of incompatibility between platforms will eventually disappear. The recent agreement between Apple and IBM to develop a common operating system is just one of several developments that will lead to a much friendlier computing environment. We can even imagine a day, perhaps a decade off, when the computer is nearly invisible to the photographer involved with electronic imaging. The computer will be part of a single plug-and-play device which will input, process, and output digital photographs.

The Chip

Modern computers would not exist without the microchip, a tiny flake of silicon, half the size of a fingernail. Also called a silicon chip or integrated circuit (IC), the chip combines the three primary components—a transistor, a capacitor, and a resistor—necessary to create electrical on/off switching. There are many different types of chips: microprocessor chips, which carry out calculations, and memory chips, which are used to store information.

Although the integrated circuit was invented in the late 1950s, it wasn't until the 1970s that ways of producing these "chips" cost-effectively were developed. Intel Corporation first developed and marketed the microprocessor chip that was able to perform a variety of computer processing functions. Today, most personal computers use microprocessor chips manufactured by Intel or Motorola. (The Macintosh and Amiga use the Motorola family of microprocessors, while IBM PCs and clones use Intel chips.)

By generating pulsing streams of electrical signals, chips produce a code, not unlike the Morse code of dots and dashes. The chip code has two signals, a high-voltage signal and a low-voltage signal. Called a binary code, it can be written down in numbers with a "1" to represent a high voltage and a "0" to represent a low voltage. The 0s and 1s in a chip's code are called bits (short for binary digits.)

Inside the chip, bits flow through the circuits in groups of 8, 16, or 32. A group of 8 bits is called a byte, which is about enough memory to store a single letter of the alphabet. These bytes move along separate "tracks" much like cars on a freeway.

(continued)

(continued)

Chips are packaged in small plastic cases with legs, called pins, which are coated with gold or tin. These pins enable them to fit into a circuit board to make a good electrical connection. They are often attached to a board called a printed circuit board (PCB). Metal tracks printed on the board's surface carry the electrical signals between the microprocessor and the other chips. Some lead to an edge connector, where other parts of the machine are plugged onto the printed circuit board.

Microprocessor chips are continuously improving and research continues to make them ever faster. For example, at this time, most chips are built around a system called CISC, which means Complex Instruction Set Computing. In the future, more and more chips will be built around a system called RISC, or Reduced Instruction Set Computing, which will make them faster yet by reducing the average complexity of a single instruction. New hardware and software will be required to take advantage of these new chips.

User Interface Devices

The most common peripheral that facilitates user interaction with a computer is the keyboard. While it is the standard input device for the average computer user, if the primary task performed on the computer is to be image manipulation, a more precise and versatile device is required. Some of the following devices are more readily available for one platform than another.

Mice. Made popular by the Macintosh, the mouse, a puck-like object, has special software that translates its movements across a table or pad into movements of a cursor (or pointer) across the screen. One or more switches (or buttons) on the top of the

(continued)

(continued)

mouse allow the user to choose and manipulate the screen images under the pointer. These devices are inexpensive ($75 to $150) and in wide use. They are not as accurate as a graphics tablet (below), and therefore have limited value in a sophisticated photographic imaging system, but are perfectly sufficient for average consumer use.

Graphics Tablets and Styli. Serious photographic image manipulation requires the use of a stylus—a pen-like device—in combination with a graphics tablet, sometimes called a graphics pad or table. These tablets range in size but generally look like thin light tables. They often contain thinly spaced wires arranged in a grid. These wires detect the exact placement of the stylus and relate the information via a cord or infrared sensor to the computer and the computer monitor. These devices are rated by their ability to discern detail. The most expensive models are able to discern up to 10,000 dots per inch (dpi), while lower-cost ones discern only 60 dpi. Some come with styli that are pressure sensitive and mimic a brush so that width or color can be varied by pressure. Some use a cordless stylus, which makes drawing much easier. One of the most popular of these devices is the Wacom tablet, available for both DOS and Macintosh machines, and used by several of the photographers featured in this book. Prices of graphics tablets range from $150 to $6,000, depending on size, resolution, and accuracy.

Apple Macintosh

The Apple Macintosh line is built around the Motorola 68000 microprocessor chip. The low-cost Mac Classic uses the 68000

(continued)

(continued)

and operates at 8 MHz and 0.35 MIPS, while the near-top-of-the-line Mac IIfx uses the 68030, operating at 40 MHz and 20 MIPS, or 50 times faster. The fastest Macintosh currently available is the Quadra series, which is not a true desktop device, but is closer to being a workstation computer. It is powered by Motorola's 68040 microprocessor and operates twice as fast as the Macintosh IIfx.

The earliest Macintosh, introduced in 1984, had only 128K of RAM, which was barely adequate. Now no Mac is shipped without at least 2 MB of RAM, and the fx and the Quadra models support up to 20 MB of RAM. The theoretical limit for future models is 4 gigabytes of RAM.

Macintoshes were never known for their expandability until the introduction of the Mac II series. Prior to that, the only way of connecting peripherals was through the SCSI or serial ports. The Mac II series uses the fast 10 MHz NuBus and comes with up to five slots for peripherals. Although this may not sound like a lot of slots, the Mac is equipped with several ports, to which peripherals such as modems and printers can be connected without using up slot space.

The DOS World

The first IBM PC was shipped with the Intel 8088 microprocessor chip. It had only 64K of RAM and no hard disk. It was good for word processing and very simple spreadsheets. In 1983 the PC XT was introduced, which had more expansion slots (from 5 to 8) and an onboard 10-MB hard drive. It also ran at 4.77 MHz. In 1984 the AT (for Advanced Technology) was introduced. AT used the Intel 80286 microprocessor and the clockspeed went from 4.77 MHz to 6 MHz for a four-fold increase in speed. Now the top-of-the-line DOS computers use the Intel 80486 chip and run at speeds of up to 40 or 50 MHz.

(continued)

(continued)

IBM no longer makes XT or AT computers. Instead they produce a line of computers called the PS/2 (for Personal System/2), which uses the 80286, 80386, and 80486 chips, as well as a different bus. They are designed to use IBM's new OS/2 operating system, but they work very well with DOS.

The design and production of DOS computers has largely been left to second parties such as Compaq, AST Research, and Tandy. Not all these clones are identical, which can create minor compatibility problems. In general the DOS world offers more peripherals than any other computer platform, even though expansion is not always easy.

Commodore Amiga

The Amiga comes in three basic models: the 500, 2000, and the 3000. Like the Macintosh, the Amiga is based on the Motorola 68000 microprocessor chip. The 3000, which is the latest, and most expensive, model, uses the 68030/882 chip running at 25 MHz. The 3000 uses a 32-bit bus (called the Zorro III), so this machine is plenty fast for image processing. It also comes with four expansion slots, as well as an SCSI interface for storage devices and scanners and several other I/Os for other peripherals.

4.

Imaging Software

At a touch of a key or a click of a mouse, a computer can be commanded to sharpen a blurry picture, convert a negative into a positive, or manipulate an image in myriad ways. This is done using a particular type of software called imaging software. Imaging software differs from other so-called "paint programs" in that it is primarily designed to manipulate or enhance scanned images, working on existing pixels rather than creating new ones. Some products on the market combine both image-processing and painting capacities.

Just about any traditional photographic task can be simulated using imaging software. In a traditional darkroom one might use a number 3 polycontrast filter to increase contrast in a black-and-white print; imaging software converts the function of the filter into a set of mathematical equations to accomplish the same task. Even a procedure that can sharpen an out-of-focus image—which has no traditional photographic counterpart—can be employed using imaging software.

In the same way, imaging software can simulate different film emulsions, different developers, toners, or retouching tools. In digital photography, the photograph is no longer fixed or immutable. The picture becomes a kinetic sculpture; if a visual idea occurs, the software can make it happen and the results are visible immediately. No longer is it necessary to explain to a lab technician, "More blue here, more red there."

One doesn't have to be a computer programmer to benefit from imaging software. In recent years, sophisticated image-processing software has become widely available for as little as $100. People with basic computer skills can master the programs in a reasonable amount of time.

Called off-the-shelf programs because of their relative simplicity, this kind of software comes in nicely designed boxes, wrapped in plastic and can be purchased at computer stores or through mail order. These programs include an instruction manual, telephone support, and often, on-line support. There is also a warranty and sometimes a money back guarantee.

Although the advantages to buying off-the-shelf software are numerous—cost, ease of use, track record—it is important to point out that developing custom software is a viable option for some photographers. The same photographers who aren't satisfied with off-the-shelf papers and developers and manufacture their own materials should explore this alternative as a way of pushing the limits of photography even further. It takes basic programming skills, of course, but more important, a clear sense of what you want from a program. "Homebrew" software programs are often passed from developer to developer via computer bulletin boards, newsletters, or user groups. Some homebrews, after lots of experimentation and system crashes, have been successfully turned into best-selling commercial products.

How Software Works

At the most basic level, a computer is really just a series of switches with two possible states: on or off. Software is a collection of instructions that tell the computer how the switches should be set. There are many levels of software "languages" but the most basic is machine language, and it is nothing except 1s and 0s. In machine language, a single instruction might be written as 1000011111000001, which the computer can read and execute in a fraction of a second. Obviously, for programmers who want to instruct a computer to perform a task, writing and com-

(continued)

(continued)

municating with massive numbers in this way is enormously time-consuming. For this reason, different ways of instructing a computer have been developed that use the English language rather than numbers.

One of these is assembly language. To translate this "language" into the numbers of machine language requires a separate program called an assembler. Higher-level languages—i.e., languages that are English-like—are quicker and easier to use than assembly language. Instead of requiring three commands to execute an instruction, for example, these languages might only require one. They also require a translator, which can be an interpreter or a compiler. The best known of these languages are BASIC, Logo, Pascal, C, and Forth.

There are basically two forms of software: software that actually performs a task, and software that contains raw data (such as words, numbers, and images) in what are called data files. Software that performs a given task can be broken down further into operating-system software, which controls the central processing unit (CPU), and application software, which is written to perform a specific task such as word processing or image enhancement.

Each computer platform has its own operating system: DOS and OS/2 are the operating systems of the IBM and IBM compatible computers, MacOS for the Macintosh and AmigaDOS for the Commodore Amiga. Although these systems are not compatible with one another, there is one operating system, called UNIX, which was designed to run on virtually any kind of computer. UNIX was developed over 20 years ago by AT&T. It's an ambitious idea, especially since the UNIX operating system takes 80 megabytes of storage just for itself. In 1982 Sun Microsystems chose UNIX for its new line of engineering workstations, geared to compete with minicomputers. Silicon Graphics and NeXT all use UNIX as their operating system as well. It is expected that as UNIX evolves, it will be used by more computer platforms.

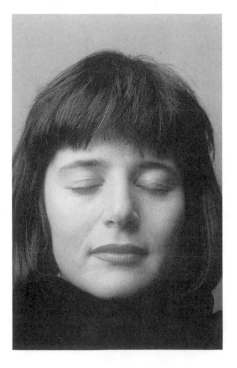

*Image-processing
software programs, like
Adobe's Photoshop, enable
the individual photographer,
working on a personal computer, to perform the kind of
creative manipulation that
has never before been
possible.* (Courtesy of
Adobe Systems)

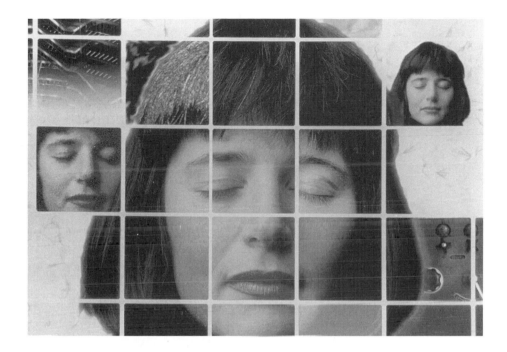

What Imaging Software Does

Most of today's off-the-shelf imaging programs attempt to create a workspace with a familiar look and feel. To some extent they rely on the image metaphors of the underlying graphical user interface, but they also make use of their own. For example, icons that represent tools such as paint brushes, scissors, and erasers can be selected to perform the functions of painting, cutting, or erasing portions of an image. By selecting from choices on a "menu," images can be rotated, contrast and brightness controlled, filters applied, and many computer-specific manipulations performed. In traditional photography, dodging, burning, and retouching take place at different stages of the photographic process. In image processing it all occurs on the video screen. With well-designed programs users can sit at a computer and execute specific tasks without much difficulty.

The seven primary functions of imaging software include:

- retouching
- color and tone correction
- cut-and-paste montaging

- image-enhancement filters
- special-effect filters
- masking
- color separations (prepress).

Not all programs include all the above functions, nor do most photographers need them. For example, some software is written specifically for color separations, which may extend the control a photographer has over how an image may be reproduced in a magazine or book but it also leaves open the possibility of theoretical and technical problems that many photographers may wish to avoid.

Retouching. Retouching with computer software involves manipulation of selected regions of an image to soften an edge, remove an unwanted artifact, or duplicate some desirable part of the image.

Some of the tools used in electronic retouching simulate the kind of work formerly performed by airbrushes and paintbrushes, except the results are observed in real time on a computer screen rather than on a hard copy. Other less familiar retouching tools are:

- cloning tools, which duplicate selected areas of an image;
- smudge tools, which create an effect much like a finger dipped in ink and touched lightly to paper;
- erasers, which easily wipe away undesirable areas;
- pattern fill, which fills a selected area with a pattern of color or design.

Color and Tone Correction. Color correction can be used to completely change the color of an object in an image, for example, changing a red car to blue, or to compensate for color shifts due to improperly exposed or developed film. Tone correction is the control of brightness, contrast, and gamma, and has much the same effect as changing paper or developer in a traditional photographic process.

Color adjustments are typically performed in one of the color spaces (discussed in more detail in Chapter 6). The most common color space is the color space of the monitor, RGB, so called because its primary components are red, green, and blue, or the color space of the printer, CYMK, an acronym for the three subtractive colors used by the printing industry—Cyan, Yellow, Magenta, plus black, which is labeled K to distinguish it from blue, which is used in primary color schemes.

An RGB or CYMK tool commonly is a set of three or four slider controls that allow the individual adjustment of the colors contained in an image. Numerical values can also be entered to create a similar effect. To change the red car to blue, for example, the various primary or subtractive colors are adjusted until desired effect is achieved. There is however, a simpler and more intuitive way of doing this: by using yet another color space, often included in imaging software, called LHS. **L**uminance is for brightness of color, **H**ue is color saturation and **S**aturation is the purity of color. Using the LHS color model to change the color of the car, contrast and saturation could be left alone while only the hue, or color saturation is changed.

To color correct an image, it is important to remember that monitors vary from model to model, from manufacturer to manufacturer, and from day to day, because of changing temperature and the aging of the phosphorous tube. In order for color correction to have any effectiveness, monitors must be carefully calibrated to an output device, either through special software or by employing hardware calibration methods.

Monitor color (on tone) correction consists of three separate control tools: brightness (which affects all the pixels equally), contrast (which affects the relationships between pixels, making an adjacent pixel, for example, brighter, while making another darker), and gamma (which is used to expand or contract certain tonal regions of an image, e.g., to bring out shadow detail). Tone correction tools are either represented graphically as slide controls or tonal values can be entered numerically.

A useful tool used to measure tonal variations in an image is a histogram. Histograms were borrowed from the science of statistics by software engineers to graphically represent frequency distributions, in this case to show the levels of contrast throughout an image. For example, high-contrast images show up as two peaks on a graph at either end of the brightness area. Low-contrast images show up as a dominant mound in one region of the graph. Dynamic range can also be measured using the histogram. If measurements show pixels falling between a small portion of gray values and none in other areas, there is small dynamic range present. A wide distribution shows a large dynamic range. This information is critical in determining proper tonal changes.

Cut-and-Paste Montaging. Cut and paste works like photo montaging with real scissors and paste. However, with electronic imaging it is possible to apply sophisticated effects with ease. For example, parts of an image can be pasted with varying degrees of transparency so that the underlining picture shows through to create ghosting effects. In addition, the edges of the pasted region can be softened to create a more seamless bond. The tools associated with this function are generally called scissors and lassos or selection tools. Typically they are represented by an icon that, once selected, puts the action into effect as the cursor is dragged across the image. Selection tools allow for either manual selection of a region (which can be very tedious if the shape is complex or big) or automatic (autotrace) selection, in which the software does the work of finding the edges of an irregular shape or area.

Graphics—such as text or geometrical shapes—can also be added to a photograph using cut-and-paste techniques. However, this process reveals one of the major limitations of many image-processing software packages. Image-processing software treats the image as a large array of individual pixels. These images are called raster or bit-mapped images and once new material has been pasted onto such an image, the region underneath the pasted selection is erased and the selection becomes a permanent part of the image. This makes photomontaging very difficult because objects must be positioned correctly the first time. Most software includes an "undo" command that lets the user remove what's been added, but it has to be done immediately. Better programs have a multiple undo command that can work backward to remove several steps of recent manipulation.

There are also software packages that combine bit-map or raster images with vector objects. Vector objects are defined by control points and mathematical equations. Shapes defined this way remain distinct from each other, even when combined. Because the image is encoded in formulas and not represented by individual bits, it can be manipulated (scaled, rotated, etc.) without any loss of data. Using vector and bit map together makes it much easier to create sophisticated photographic montages and subsequently edit the components by moving them around even after they have been cut and pasted.

Image-Enhancement Filters. Image-enhancement filters are typically designed to apply a mathematical equation that filters in or out such effects that can, for example, "sharpen" or "smooth" the image or selected parts of the image. More sophisticated filters can mathematically detect degraded regions of an image—for example, too light, too dark, under- or overexposed, motion blur or excessive video noise—and apply a correction to these regions.

Special-Effect Filters. Special-effect filters are typically designed to create unusual geometrical distortions, as well as special effects such as a mezzotint look, blurs, and star bursts. One geometrical filter makes an image act as if it were printed on a sheet of rubber. The "rubber image" can be twisted or distorted into any number of shapes. Parallax lens corrections can also be simulated using this kind of software, mathematically duplicating the view camera's swings, tilts, and lifts.

Masking. Since many functions of image processing are permanent and irreversible, some software programs allow the creation of electronic masks or friskets that selectively protect parts of the image from the applied operation. For example, the first step in an airbrushing operation might be to create masks to protect all the areas of an image except the one to be retouched.

Creating masks requires a lot of internal computer memory but some computer operating systems and display boards support what is called a special "Alpha channel" that can be used to create masks or, alternatively, to create text or graphic overlays in the image without using any extra internal memory. They are able to do this because they support 32 bits per pixel—since most monitors only display 24 bits per pixel, an extra 8 bits per pixel are left for the alpha channel.

Color Separations (Prepress). Color separation is discussed in detail in Chapter 6, "Output and Prepress," but at its simplest level it provides a translation for the RGB color space of the monitor to the CYMK color space of the printer. It can also provide output to a digital typesetter or directly to high-end prepress systems.

Image View Controls

There are many controls available for determining the way an image is viewed on a monitor. Rotating or flip controls are especially handy if an image is accidentally scanned at an odd angle. Large images, which take up more space than the monitor can display, can be selectively viewed by scroll or pan controls. By zooming in on an image, a small portion of a screen can be magnified to the individual pixel level for extremely precise editing.

File Format

File formats are determined by the way the computer and software organize their information. Most imaging software accept a variety of formats, but the most common file format is TIFF, or Tagged Image File Format. Some of the other formats include PICT, RIFF (Raster Image File Format), PCK, BMP, and EPS (Encapsulated PostScript).

In an ideal world there would only be one file format to specify the way an image should be represented. The multifile world exists because the software technology used in imaging systems has been developed over the years by different vendors simultaneously.

To some extent, the problems of compatibility among file formats, software applications, and different computer platforms, can be avoided by the use of file translator software. This can turn, say, an Amiga file into a TIFF file read by both Macs and PCs. These file translators are not always perfectly successful, however. To make things even more confusing, not all TIFF files are the same. In theory, Macintosh software will open a DOS TIFF file, but for reasons only known to individual programmers, this doesn't always happen.

Software Versions

Software packages are constantly being upgraded. The first version of a software package is usually labeled v 1.0. As the software grows, adapting to new hardware and incorporating more features, the version number becomes greater. A small change will be denoted by an incremental increase to, say, version 1.2. Larger changes are represented by larger numbers to the left of the decimal point. The latest version is generally the one to buy and the surest way to find out the latest version number is to call the publisher directly. By sending the software registration card back to the publisher one is informed when new versions are released. These upgrades are usually available to registered users for a nominal charge.

Buying Advice

One of the most inexpensive ways to buy software is through mail-order firms that advertise in special-interest magazines. The disadvantage of this is the lack of a local dealer to answer the inevitable questions that arise. In the case of software, however, access to a dealer may not be necessary, since many software companies provide on-line or telephone support for registered owners.

Software is bought primarily for its unique features, but there are two other factors, which are often overlooked: its speed and efficiency. This is something quite different from the processing speed of the computer (which of course makes a difference in how fast a program will operate). The sluggishness with which a program opens a file may seem a minor annoyance, but in complex operations, such as cutting and pasting, speed can make a big difference. Unfortunately operating speed is a variable that is hard to quantify, especially since programs run at different speeds on different computers. The best way to verify a program's true operating speed is to test the software in a real-life situation. Many computer magazines operate testing labs that do this for you and publish the results. In Part Four, "The Resources," is an annotated listing of selected off-the-shelf software packages that are available.

5.

Digitizers and Scanners

Scanners and digitizers—the terms are nearly synonymous—are translators. They convert traditional photographic images, video, and electronic still images into computer language that enables these images to be processed by the computer. Some scanners can even be used on stationary three-dimensional objects.

Scanners, which function much like a copy camera or copy machine, are used in the studio, office, or electronic darkroom. Like most copy cameras they are fixed devices and generally have greater lighting and power requirements than hand-held cameras. In order to be fully operational, they must be physically hooked up to a computer with special cables through which they receive most of their instructions. In computer parlance they are part of a category of hardware called peripherals, which also includes printers, mice, cameras, or any add-on devices not necessary to basic computer operation.

The best digitizers, which are capable of very precise duplication of slides and prints, cost over $100,000 and are used by major printing and publishing concerns. In recent years, however, lower-cost digitizers and scanners have appeared. Prices now range from $200 to $20,000 with the resulting reproduction quality ranging from poor to very good. For individual photographers interested in digital imaging, the positive trend toward lower hardware prices and higher output quality is expected to continue.

There are different types of scanners available to photographers. Scanners differ according to function—some are specifically made for color work, others for monochrome. Some low-end scanners, like Kodalith film, have limits on their ability to discern tonal values and are primarily used to scan line art that contains few middle tones.

The ability of a scanner or digitizer to accurately render an image depends upon its ability to resolve the bits of information the image contains. This ability is rated in three ways, with a higher number being better than a lower one: the raw ability to discern the image is rated in dots per inch (or dpi); the ability to discern the shade or tone of the resolved dot is rated in bits per dot (usually expressed just as bits); the ability to discern color is simply rated as yes or no.

The resolution of low-end scanners ranges from 100 to 1,000 dpi, with 200 to 400 being the most prevalent. Medium-range scanners can resolve from 300 to 1,200 dpi, and the high-end is anything beyond 1,200 dpi.

Low-end scanners resolve their dots as either on or off—there is no such thing as gray or color. Grays are approximated by the spacing of the dot pattern—more dots are darker, fewer dots are lighter. For scanning line art containing no grays or shading, a low-end scanner is perfectly adequate.

Medium-range monochrome scanners, called grayscale scanners, are capable of grading each dot with 8, 16, 24, or 32 bits of information. The most common grayscale scanners are 400 to 600 dpi, 8-bit or 24-bit units that can deliver a continuous tone shift from black to white. A 24-bit grayscale scanner at 600 dpi comfortably exceeds print image quality, and is frequently acceptable for medium-grade photographic proofs.

Medium-range color scanners are 24-bit or 32-bit units with resolutions of 300 to 1,000 dpi. 24-bit, 400 dpi color images are frequently used in computer and other commercial magazines (after professional color separations).

High-end scanners and digitizers can faithfully reproduce color film at resolutions exceeding 3,500 dpi, and with 36-bit accuracy (68 billion colors). Many high-end scanners and digitizers consist of a hardware/software combination that is also capable of compressing the stored image—a high-resolution image of a 35mm positive slide would otherwise occupy more than 70 megabytes of storage space.

Most low- to medium-level scanners come with an added bonus: Optical Character Recognition (OCR) software—programs that can decipher text from a scanned or faxed bit-mapped image.

How much resolution you will need is entirely dependent on what you will be doing with the scanned image. For more information, see the Scan Resolution Formula section later in this chapter.

Here is a rundown of the scanners and digitizers that the average photographer will encounter, as well as an explanation of the more exotic high-end systems that are found in large professional publishing operations.

Flatbed Scanners

By far the most common scanners, flatbeds look and act much like a common office copier. They employ a light source to illuminate a two-dimensional object or photograph, some sort of sensing device, and a step motor to move the sensor and light source. The image is placed face down on the glass bed of the scanner. Using the software that comes with the scanner, the photographer uses the computer to direct the scanning head to read the image and convert it into a digital file on the computer.

Advantages: Flatbed scanners have become a common tool for graphic artists, designers, architects, and other professionals involved with desktop publishing and presentation graphics. They are competitively priced and available in a variety of specifications. Generally, they are easy to set up and use, and are relatively inexpensive. Flatbeds are medium-end scanners and are usually either grayscale or grayscale/color capable. As such they are ideal for OCR and line art, and are acceptable for some types of photographic work. They work well in a network/work group environment.

Disadvantages: They take up valuable space on the desktop and, without special attachments, cannot scan transparencies, negatives, or 3D objects.

How They Work: Flatbed scanners work like document copiers. An image (maximum $11'' \times 14''$ in size) is placed on the glass and covered with a light shielding lid. A light source (usually a fluorescent light) reflects light off the image and back to an array of CCD light-sensitive cells. The desired dpi, and image enlargement or reduction, are set by software. Most color scanners require the scan head to make three passes, one each for red, green, and blue. The three values are combined into a full-color picture that is displayed on the monitor. The entire process takes about 30 seconds for black and white, a few minutes for color. Processing time can vary somewhat from brand to brand and depending on the processing speed of your computer and its configuration.

Film Scanners

Desktop film or slide scanners function much like slide projectors. The slide or negative is put in a carrier or slide holder and taken into the machine. A light source projects the slide onto a sensor, which translates it into digital data. Of all the scanners available, film scanners are the most useful to the professional photographer today, but they are also among the most costly, running in the thousands of dollars.

Advantages: Slides or negatives are easier to handle, store, and transport than prints. Slides have a wider range of brightness and color saturation than reflective materials such as color prints. Prints are also expensive and time-consuming to make. If a print can be avoided, time and money is saved. As the demand grows for these scanners more manufacturers will enter the market and prices will inevitably drop.

Disadvantages: The actual cost of film scanners is high and there are hidden costs as well. Color scanning inherently requires expensive storage devices to hold the large image files generated and powerful personal computers to process all that information. A pricey video display card is almost essential, as well as a color monitor. Time-consuming color corrections must also be considered because these scanners are generally not calibrated for all types of film. In theory, film scanners scan both negative and transparency film. In practice, however, because of the inherent orange mask in negative film and the necessity of having to reverse the tones for display, they do so with some difficulty. It is expected that this differential will be minimized or eliminated in time, however.

How They Work: Before the first use (and periodically after) many slide/film scanners, as well as other scanners, must be calibrated to establish values for absolute black and absolute white, and to compensate for variations in the lighting. Even the projection light source, as it ages, creates variations in the color scan that must be corrected by frequent calibration.

It is always prudent to first make a low-resolution preview scan. This takes from 30 to 60 seconds and is useful for making any cropping and gamma correction (which establishes the darkest and lightest points of the image and allows the scanner software to make optimal use of the 8-bit-per-pixel dynamic range of the scanner).

Then an actual, full-resolution scan is made, which takes from 2 to 10 minutes, depending on the resolution. Most desktop scanners use a one-dimensional CCD array. Either the CCD or the film is moved in relation to the other to complete the scan.

Video Digitizers

These devices convert electronic signals from VCRs, video cameras, still video cameras, laser disc players, and broadcast TV into digital form. In the case of moving images, a still frame is grabbed and then converted into digital data.

Video digitizers are peripheral devices that sit between a video source and the computer. Some video digitizers are separate, sophisticated peripherals that perform a number of functions other than image digitizing, but are relevant to publishing and telecommunications. Some newspapers, for example, use a high-end video digitizer to grab still pictures off a live TV news feed, and instantly convert it to a digital image file, which then can be sent direct to a press or sent via telephone lines to another location for output. Other simpler video digitizers can be reduced to circuit boards that can be fitted into the computer itself. These latter are of use to individual photographers.

Advantages: They create a bridge between the digital world of computers and the analog (i.e., non-digtial) world of video.

Disadvantages: A video digitizer is only one part of a link that includes a video source, a computer, and a monitor. To make all the components work together is often tricky, especially in an IBM or MS-DOS–compatible environment where hundreds of different configurations of computers and peripherals exist. Also, since most electronic signals are tied into the American (NTSC) or European (PAL or SECAM) television standard, the resolution of the image is limited by the relatively small amount of information in a moving image. (A comparison is the image quality of a single frame of a 35mm movie to that of a 35mm slide.)

How They Work: The video image actually starts as an electronic signal. Except for the still video camera, most of the images are "in motion," moving at the speed of one frame every ¹⁄₃₀th of a second. An image must therefore be "grabbed" using the frame grabber component of a digitizer board—essentially a snapshot of an entire video frame. Then the signal is digitized and converted into one of a variety of standard formats that the computer can read.

Some of the less expensive digitizers don't have a frame grabber feature and can only take images from a static source, such as a still video camera.

Video Camera Scanners

Very often these scanners look like copy cameras, except that a video camera is mounted on the stand instead. The electronic signal from the camera must still be converted from its analog (i.e., non-digital) form using a frame-grabbing video digitizer that is installed in the computer.

Advantages: Many of these scanners use industrial quality video cameras, with high quality. The images look terrific on the monitor screen and are excellent (albeit expensive) as proofing devices. Often they come bundled with dedicated video digitizer boards, making their setup easier. They enable the user to make digital images of large, three-dimensional objects, such as still-life pictures or standard studio product shots.

Disadvantages: The signal from these cameras is analog and some quality is lost when it is converted into digital form. Also, they are more expensive than consumer video cameras and require carefully positioned and balanced external lighting.

How They Work: The more expensive video cameras contain two-dimensional image sensors, typically CCDs that convert light intensities into red, green, and blue (RGB) and luminance signals. In a less expensive version that employs a consumer camera these signals are encoded into NTSC (or PAL or SECAM) and stored directly on video tape by a video recorder built into the camera. These formats are made for broadcast television and compress or reduce much of the information in the video signal for more efficient transmission and inherently produce images of lower quality.

Hand-held Scanners

These low- to medium-level scanners are noted for their low price. They are useful for someone who wants to put an occasional small, low- to medium-grade image into a computer-generated document. The hand-held scanner resembles a vacuum cleaner attachment (the one for drapery). The approximately 4-inch-wide head, containing the light source and sensor, is dragged across the image to be scanned.

Advantages: Hand-held scanners go where other scanners can't: they scan images and graphics from hefty books; they can even pick up fabric patterns off upholstery. They take up less space, and in a world of exploding peripherals and shrinking desktops, that's important. Perhaps the best argument in their favor is they cost significantly less than other scanners, ranging in price from $150 to $900. Hand-held scanners are most useful when output requirements are for low- to medium-resolution images and of limited size. Hand-held scanners also have a place in high-end publishing: their scans can be manipulated so that they resemble line art or sketches and the output can be used like photostats in the page layouts of desktop publishing software applications (such as Aldus's Pagemaker program) where they are used to represent the final image during design. When the layout is finalized higher resolution scans can be substituted.

Disadvantages: Hand-held scanners have improved since they were first introduced in the mid-1980s. They now scan 24-bit color and 8-bit grayscale, and have gone from 200 dpi to 400 dpi. But much of this technology can be undone by shaky, unpredictable movement of the operator's hand, which moves the light-sensitive elements across the image. It takes a good deal of practice to get consistently good images—the software can usually correct for skew, but not for irregular movement.

The size of the scan can be inconvenient, even with special software that allows multiple scans to be combined. At this time, the widest horizontal area that any hand-held scanner can make in a single pass is 4.2 inches. The vertical dimension of the scan can be much larger and is usually determined by the amount of available memory in the computer.

How They Work: All hand-held scanners operate in a similar fashion. They have a scanning head variously designed to fit in the operator's hand. Inside are a daylight balanced light source, mirrors to reflect the image back to a sensor (CCD), and electronics to move the information in digital form to the computer.

A roller inside the head measures the motion across the image and tells the scanner when to sample new lines of information. Some of the devices have manual controls such as start scan, lighten and darken, bright and normal, resolution options, and halftone dot size control. A cord connects the scanning head to either an SCSI box (for the Mac or Amiga) or to an adaptor card for the PC.

Scanning is done by grasping the scan head, pushing the start button on the scanner, and slowly pulling the head across an image. Most display the result in real time on the screen, some in dithered form, others in grays or in color. Some scanners come with sensors that tell you if you are scanning too fast and producing distortion (which may be desirable for special effects).

Overhead Scanners

Most overhead scanners employ a scanning head mounted on a small tower. The scanning head, along with a light source, mechanically sweeps over a baseboard where photographs or artwork lie face up. Some overhead scanners (like the Array scanner) look and function more like an enlarger, with the scan head focused and vertically adjusted by hand.

Advantages: They can handle low-profile, three-dimensional objects as well as two-dimensional photographs. Since the photograph is facing up —rather than down as with the flatbed scanners— it is easier to position. Some overhead scanners combine the features of a digital camera, a slide and film scanner, and a flatbed scanner.

Disadvantages: Like video camera scanners, overhead scanners require an external light source that must be carefully positioned and color balanced.

How They Work: Some overhead scanners—such as the Truvel TZ-3— use micromotors to move a scanning head. A built-in light moves with the head. The scan head consists of the same linear CCDs used in flatbed scanners. Color images require three passes of the sensor head. The Array scanner is the only scanner that uses an area array of photo diodes and oscillating crystals that move the array in submicron increments. This unique scanning technique—moving an area array of photo diodes rather than a linear CCD—extends the capacity of the sensor, for example, allowing it to collect 12 bits of data per color pixel and increase the dynamic range nearly to the range of a high-end drum scanner. However, because the "snapshots" it takes have to be "patched" together with software, magnification reveals a processed look.

Sheetfed Scanners

Sheetfed scanners look and work much like a FAX machine. Two-dimensional images are fed through rollers and pass by a scanning head. They are generally used to convert paper text into electronic files by running the scanned image through OCR software. These scanners have very limited functions for photographic or other graphic applications.

There are, however, very inexpensive devices that ingeniously turn a dot matrix printer into a sheetfed scanner, which—purely because of their low cost—may have some value to a photographer. To do this, specially designed modules are fitted in place of the printer's print-head. The image to be scanned is attached to the printer's paper scroll and is fed through the paper tractor until the top of the image lines up with the scanning module. When activated by the software, the module moves slowly back and forth across the image and activates the printer to move the image up after each pass.

Advantages: Sheetfed scanners are slightly cheaper than flatbed scanners and take up less space. They are especially good for OCR scanning.

Disadvantages: There are severe limitations as to what can be scanned—the picture must fit in between the rollers and within the width of the sheet and must be made of a material that is flexible enough to bend around the rollers. Photographs printed on glossy paper often slip in the rollers ruining the orientation of the image.

How They Work: Except for the fact that images are rolled past a scanning head, these scanners contain the same circuitry and components as the flatbed scanners and therefore work the same.

Drum Scanners

Drum scanners represent the high end of scanning technology and they are priced accordingly. They are often huge machines and they require a highly skilled operator. Some of the drum scanners are so sensitive that they are required to be in a climate-controlled room. They are capable of accepting all sorts of media, however, and although they are extremely expensive, access is becoming more readily available through service bureaus.

Advantages: The highest possible dynamic range in a photograph can be rendered by a drum scanner. Some are so powerful that they can reveal information that the photographer would be unable to see with the naked eye. These high-end production units are oriented toward high-volume professional publishing. As you would expect, they are able to achieve the highest quality and fastest speed in scanning today. While access to this technology by individual users has been limited, it is increasing because of new technologies that allow these high-end systems to interface with PC and Apple computers via the proliferation of service bureaus.

Disadvantages: Price and difficulty of use make individual ownership unlikely. These systems start at over $50,000 and can run into the millions. The people who operate them are highly trained with years of experience. Only such qualified personnel are allowed to run these systems and a photographer whose work is being scanned on them must convey his instructions and creative decisions to the operator in person or through detailed instructions.

How They Work: Reflective or transmittive art (a print or a slide) is taped on a circular plexiglass drum. The drum revolves and a lamp within the drum focuses a minute spot of laser light onto the original. A lens, scanning the horizontal axis of the drum, focuses the light through three color separation filters—red, green, and blue. Each filter is attached to a photomultiplier, which converts the light into electrical pulses.

Many of these units combine scanning with film writing. If color correction, cropping or black generation are the only adjustments required, the electronic signals may remain in analog form throughout the process. The analog representation of the image is displayed on a large-screen monitor and the colors are manipulated. But if spatial manipulation or airbrushing (retouching) is required, the analog signal must be converted into digital format and routed to a sophisticated computer for manipulation with the appropriate software.

The resulting scan is typically 50 megabytes or more, depending on the size that the image will run in print. Such a large amount of digital information precludes its running on a desktop computer—it requires a workstation computer or larger.

Most of the scanning on these units is done to generate the color separations necessary for printing the quality images you see today in large metropolitan newspapers, magazines or for direct mail promotional advertisements and displays. The printing industry has been using digital photography for some years now, but it is only recently that the technology has migrated back toward the creators of the images to complete the digital revolution.

Choosing a Scanner

At some point a photographer will buy a scanner, borrow a colleague's, or use a service bureau. In all cases, it is the final use of the image—how big it will be reproduced, at what level of quality, etc.—that will determine the type of scanner needed. If the final destination of a scanned image is a TV monitor (for use in a multimedia presentation) or a low-resolution print (via a laser printer for reproduction in a newsletter, etc.), most scanners—even ones under $300—will provide images of suitable quality.

There are numerous scanners that meet the criteria for obtaining the quality required for black-and-white newspaper or magazine reproduction. They cost between $500 and $3,000. (Low-level color scanners, which can be useful for making composite sketches, called "comps," for desktop design but which have limited use outside of comps, can also be found for this price.)

If a photographer is interested in converting hundreds of images into a low-resolution inventory of work (for digital stock or a visual data base), the only alternative is the video digitizer combined with a video camera. Not only is this method quick—less than a second for a 35mm slide—but the storage requirements per image are not high.

Matching the quality of traditional silver-based prints or transparencies with a digital image requires scanners that typically cost well over the budget of most individual photographers. To achieve that level of quality requires desktop film scanners or drum scanners. Unless you have an ongoing need for high-quality scans and can justify the cost of a desktop scanner, using one at an electronic publishing service bureau is the best alternative.

Scanner Terms and Technology

Since scanners are complex devices that come with varying degrees of technical sophistication, here are some of the more important details to keep in mind when considering the use or purchase of a scanner.

Service Bureaus—the Pro Labs of the Future

Service bureaus are small businesses that have sprung up in recent years to serve the prepress graphic arts industry as it moves toward electronic imaging. They function much like a professional photo lab. Instead of a Kodachrome or an E-6 processing line, there is a sophisticated drum scanner with a computer workstation attached. In this case the output is not Kodak's yellow box of slides but a magnetic disk or tape containing the digital representations of the photographic images.

These service bureaus range from small shops handling the needs of desktop publishers to large operations serving ad agencies and professional publishing houses. Like the differences between a one-hour photo and a professional's custom lab, the quality, services and prices vary accordingly. Depending on the photographer's client's needs and the budget allowed, an entire range of these services is available.

At a corner service bureau, photographers are apt to walk in off the street and get a scan while they wait. Some may even perform the scans themselves after some instruction using the bureau's desktop scanner.

At the other extreme is the professional prepress service bureau where an appointment is required and time is billed at hundreds of dollars an hour. A skilled operator is required to operate the machinery and the billing units vary according to the time required to complete the task and its complexity. Many professional photo labs, which specialize in serving advertising photographers and their agency clients, have already begun to invest in sophisticated drum scanner technology and the associated image-processing tasks like digital retouching.

Most photographers will be able to achieve the results they need at a local service bureau using a desktop system. A reminder, however: The higher the quality of the scan means that more image detail has been translated into digital data. The

(continued)

> *(continued)*
>
> more data, the larger the image file. Some desktop slide scanners, if set to maximum resolution, can convert a 35mm slide into a digital file that could weigh in at 70 megabytes of data.
>
> Trying to manipulate such a large body of data slows most personal computers to a crawl. "Crunching" such large data files is impractical, not the best use of a personal computer, and should be avoided.

Bits per Pixel. Scanners work by electronically breaking down an image into a fine mesh of pixels. Think of each pixel as a box. The amount of information contained in each box (or pixel) is determined by how many bits, or levels of tones, the scanner is capable of recording. If a pixel only contains one bit of information (2^1), it means it contains only two levels of information. In a sense it is a flat box, capable only of reading black or white.

More bits per pixel means more levels of gray between black and white can be represented and thus a finer grade image is rendered. A two-bit scanner will register four levels of gray (i.e., 2^2) per pixel. Three bits records eight levels (2^3), and so on. (See diagram.) Generally, the ability to record 256 levels of gray (2^8, the product of an 8-bit scanner) is considered a starting point for any serious scanning.

The measurement of bits per pixel is a difficult concept to grasp and increasingly, as scanners are mass marketed, manufacturers use instead a ratings system based on numbers of gray. This can be misleading. Information from a 1-bit scanner (whose hardware sees only two values—black and white) or a 2-bit scanner (four values) can be extrapolated by software so that many more values of a gray are simulated. This mathematical trick is accomplished by using a software technique called dithering. An 8-bit grayscale scanner (hardware) is the absolute minimum acceptable gradation (256 true levels) for scanning black-and-white photographic images. A 24-bit color scanner (hardware) is the absolute minimum acceptable gradation (256 true levels for each of the three colors, red, green, and blue) for scanning color photographic images. Software can help, but it cannot take the place of adequate raw information.

Dithering. There are many ways to dither a digital image but the purpose is always to extend or average the limited information available. It's also a way of overcoming the limits of the hardware and keeping the price of the equipment down.

In some cases dithering means using clusters of pixels to form dots whose individual size and shape represent gray values. Seen from a distance these clusters give an impression of gray—much like the halftone dots in newspaper and magazine reproduction.

Another dithering technique averages the values between two pixels and generates an appropriate pixel, which makes the transition between pixels smoother and the image more photo-like. (Dithering color is similar but far more complex.)

Dithering is very useful because it optimizes the imaging capability of the hardware. But a dithered image is such a complex latticework of real and imagined values that it is almost impossible to edit or resize. When manipulated, it "pixelizes" into artificial patterns and clumps that can be likened to such creative darkroom techniques as solarization. A dithered image is never as good as an image scanned at higher levels.

Dots per Inch, dpi. Dpi is a standard in the traditional printing trade and refers to the dots of ink you see when you look at a newspaper or magazine with a loupe. Technically, scanners create pixels by sampling lines of a continuous-tone image. Most desktop models scan at a spatial resolution of 300 dpi, which creates an image consisting of 300 pixels per inch horizontally by 300 pixels per inch vertically.

What does that mean in terms of quality? A traditional photograph printed in a newspaper contains 85 dpi, most consumer and trade magazine images are printed at about 130 dpi. Book publishing, depending on the quality of the paper stock, can utilize 150 dpi and up. Note that the more bits per pixel, the better the image appears. The term "lines per inch," lpi, is often used by traditional printers instead of dpi, but for our purposes they mean essentially the same thing.

In practice, depending on the final output dimensions, most scanners are adequate for publication quality. (See Scan Resolution Formula below.) To compare digital scans with traditional photographic quality is problematic, however. It depends if you are talking about 35mm T-Max 3200 quality or Kodachrome 25 quality, whether it's adequate to be seen in contact sheet or if it needs to be a 16×20 print.

Scan Speed. This is an important consideration if you are scanning a lot of images. There is nothing more frustrating than waiting for a slow scanner to plod along, tying up your computer while you can do nothing else but sit and wait. A reasonable scan speed for a typical 35mm color slide, outputted at magazine or newspaper resolution, is about three minutes.

Several factors determine the speed it takes a scanner to convert a photograph into digital data. Largely, it is a function of the scanning head's sensitivity, hardware circuitry, and the method used to connect the computer to the scanner. An extremely fast method of transferring data between systems is the SCSI, a special dedicated cable and port system. A slower method is through a serial interface. (The interface capability is dependent on the type of computer you have and whether it can be adapted to the more efficient SCSI interface.) The size and resolution of the scan are other factors of scan speed.

Since there are so many variables, scan speed is not listed as a product specification and the only way of determining if a scanner is fast enough for you is to try it out using a representative sample of the kind of images you will most commonly scan. Be sure the scanner is connected to a computer that is comparable to yours and that you output the test images at the resolution that you anticipate you will require. One type of scanner that is inherently faster than all others, however, is the video digitizer, which scans most images in just seconds. On the other hand, the amount of digital information it can gather is limited and is far less than that of the higher end film scanners.

Type of Sensor. Almost all consumer scanners use solid-state sensing devices (CCDs). Drum scanners for the most part use photomultiplier tubes, an older, more tested technology, which can operate faster and with higher dynamic range capabilities than other sensors. Video cards don't contain sensors because the signal has already been converted into electrical form by another source.

Color Considerations. Scanners capable of reproducing color images work in one of two ways: three sequential scans are made through three separate color filters of red, green, and blue, then software combines the three pictures to make one color-accurate picture; or filters are placed over the photodiodes of the CCDs so that only one scan is necessary. Because sequential scanners have been on the market for a longer period, they dominate the color desktop scanner field.

When you consider that a single 35mm Kodachrome 64 slide contains as many as a million colors you begin to sense the enormity of the task of digital color imaging. As with chemical-based imaging, the technology of color is more complicated than black-and-white. Within the realm of digital photography, the technology of how color is represented—called color science—is perhaps the most complicated area in digital imaging. Color on a computer has made great strides since the early days when only eight colors were possible on a PC. Within a few years that number zoomed to over 16 million.

Many of the variables associated with color scanning are related to differences in monitors and printers. Also, the various color films used for output each have a characteristic color and density response. The issues of color calibration and of maintaining color fidelity, independent of the system or device that displays the image, are being addressed every day. Eventually the technology that accomplishes all this will be buried within the hardware, where it will work unobtrusively in the background. In the meantime, becoming familiar with and using image-processing software programs such as Adobe's Photoshop to color-balance and enhance scanned images is essential.

Scanner Software

The primary function of scanning software is to control the optical, electronic and mechanical functions of the scanner. But that's not enough. Good software includes:

- an ability to save the image in a variety of generic formats (TIFF and PICT are acronyms given to two of these formats) that can then be read or understood by different image-enhancing software applications.
- the ability to save the image to disk rather than to the computer's memory. Large-image files will quickly exceed the available RAM of most computers and must be saved on the hard disk.
- a preview option that gives a quick, low-resolution view of the image to allow cropping and density correction.
- the ability to crop an image by selecting a portion of it using a framing device or by typing in margin settings.
- brightness, contrast, and color balance controls.
- image scaling, whereby the image can be scanned at a percentage

greater or smaller than the original, effectively enlarging or reducing it.

    ▪ a tool that allows you to manipulate the image's gamma curve for precise tonal control. (A gamma curve is a nonlinear way of measuring tonal values.)

Buyer Beware

Unfortunately, a scanner's product specifications don't always tell the whole story. Several computer magazines have sophisticated labs that test and publicize a product's true line resolution, grayscale and color, scan speed, and software stability. On the other hand, as with cameras and lenses, it's best to determine a scanner's quality by independent testing.

    A good place to find independent opinions is at the meetings of local computer user groups, some of which also issue very competent and knowledgeable monthly journals. User groups tend to attract many of the most informed and generous computer people in the area. Within these societies are subgroups dedicated to particular applications or hardware where you can gather unbiased, practical information and guidance. (See Part Four, "The Resources.")

Scanning Tips

Scanning, like traditional photographic printmaking, requires lots of experimentation. While the hardware and software do most of the work, there are some things that you can do to ensure the best possible scan is realized from your photograph. Recognizing that the setup differs from hand-held scanners to flatbeds to video digitizers, here are some tips.

    Start with a well-exposed and well-printed photograph. (If scanning from a halftone source, expect strange repetitive patterns called moire (pronounced: mwa-RAY), which are caused by divergent angles of the CCDs and the halftone dots. This anomaly can be corrected by moving the image on the scanner and rescanning, scanning it slightly out of focus, or with image-processing software at a later time.) When using overhead scanners care must be given to the setup: use even, nonglare lighting, set at 45° angles.

    It's not a disaster if an image is scanned at the wrong angle, because most imaging software will correct it. However, because rotating an image requires intense mathematical calculation, and is therefore very time-consuming, it is almost always faster just to rescan with the horizon line adjusted to the angle you want.

The objective in scanning is to match the dpi of the scanned image as closely as possible to the eventual reproduction size (in halftone dots), and yet to keep the image file as small and manageable as possible. (See Scan Resolution Formula below.) By knowing beforehand the resolution

Scan Resolution Formula

There is a simple formula for calculating the resolution at which you should scan your original photograph. All you need to know is the size and resolution at which the image will be printed. (The resolution will depend on the type of printer or film recorder you intend to use.)

What happens if you don't follow this formula? If you scan at an inadequate resolution, the image will look soft or out of focus when reproduced. If you scan at a resolution higher than you need, you don't gain detail or quality, and in fact, you waste valuable storage space and processing time.

To determine the necessary dpi scanner setting you should use, multiply the width of the intended output by two and then divide by the width of the original.* Then multiply by the intended output resolution (for newspaper reproduction the output resolution will be 85 dpi, for most magazines it is 133 dpi).

$$\frac{2 \times \text{width of intended output}}{\text{width of original}} \times \text{output resolution} = \frac{\text{necessary}}{\text{dpi}}$$

(Length can be substituted for width to achieve the same results.)

*The multiplier "two" is derived from a formula called the Nyquist Criterion (also known as the Sampling Theorem), which ensures the proper resolution.

(continued)

(continued)

For example, lets start with a $4'' \times 5''$ print that is taller than it is wide. (Let's assume that it is a portrait of the type handed out with publicity releases.) The image is to be reproduced in a magazine, in a one-column layout (with a column width being 1.875 inches), with an output resolution of 133 dpi (a common printing resolution for magazines). Using the formula, we see that a scanner setting of 125 dpi is required.

$$\frac{2 \times 1.875 \text{ inches}}{4 \text{ inches}} \times 133 \text{ dpi} = 124.6 \text{ dpi}$$

Since the maximum scan resolution of most flatbed scanners is 400 dpi, this is easily achieved.

As another example, let us assume that our original is a landscape that was taken with a 35mm camera and we wish to output it as a $4'' \times 5''$ image at magazine-level resolution. Knowing that the width of a slide is about 1.38 inches, the calculation becomes:

$$\frac{2 \times 5 \text{ inches}}{1.38 \text{ inches}} \times 133 \text{ dpi} = 964 \text{ dpi}$$

Since we are enlarging this image by over 100 percent, considerably more detail will need to be captured than in the previous example. To achieve this quality, a scanner with a higher resolution capability is required. This enlargement exceeds the resolving power of many flatbed scanners, but it is well within the resolution level of desktop slide scanners.

What if the image source is video, as from a still video camera, and a digitizer board is used to get the image into the computer? This creates another scenario since, in video, the input resolution is fixed. Therefore, there is a theoretical maximum size to the output before quality becomes an issue. (Instead of the garbage-in/garbage-out maxim of the computer world, we have a silk purse/sow's ear metaphor. We can't make a beautiful image, rich in detail, with only a limited amount of color information.)

(continued)

(continued)

Since the standard American video image has to fit within the technical parameters of the TV sets manufactured in North America, these video images typically have a useful image size with approximately 400 lines of resolution. Therefore the criterion in video-to-digital image conversion is output size. Thus, when you are creating a digital image that originated as a video image, the formula becomes:

$$\frac{\text{input resolution}}{2 \times \text{output resolution}} = \text{output size}$$

Based on experiments conducted within the newspaper industry, which has done much of the pioneering work in the use of digital photography, it is felt that a factor of at least two must be used to insure satisfactory image quality in video-to-digital image conversion. This suggests that a newspaper wishing to print a still video image at an 85-line screen, should not try to print the image any larger than:

$$\frac{400 \text{ lines}}{2 \times 85 \text{ dpi}} = 2.35 \text{ inches}$$

Having to run an image this small would limit any publication. In practice, newspapers often drop the theoretical factor of 2, allowing them to print images up to approximately five inches in height with varying degrees of success, depending on the need for and the newsworthiness of the picture. A discerning reader will always be able to pick out a color image in a newspaper or newsmagazine that was grabbed from a TV by its poor quality, softness, and lack of dynamic range in the color. Editors are aware of this problem, but in a fast-breaking news situation having an image is more important than image quality. Photojournalists recognize that readers are more interested in seeing the event portrayed and less concerned with the method of its portrayal.

required in the final reproduction of the photograph, both operator time and storage space will be optimized.

Always keep in mind that what you see on a screen is not always what you'll get in output. As when developing a print under darkroom lighting—where you have to learn how to make evaluations and adjust exposure and development time for each combination of film, negative density, paper, and darkroom chemistry—each hardware and software setup affects digital output in a unique way. Learn to interpret the image on the screen so that you can employ the proper software controls to guarantee the output you want each time.

There are no easy solutions to this; you develop an ability to judge the effects of your manipulations only through practice. Fortunately, about the only cost of such experiments is your time. Unsatisfactory scans can be trashed with no waste and little guilt. The digital image is nothing more than a mathematical equation residing on your computer's hard disk. This image file can be easily purged, if necessary, and the space reclaimed to hold another image file.

The Future of Scanners

With the rapid and constant changes in electronic imaging, and the creation of more sophisticated and less expensive electronic cameras, it is correct to ask whether it is necessary to invest in a scanner at all.

Eastman Kodak's new Photo CD technology, while aimed at the consumer snapshooter, has implications for photographers interested in digital imaging. The Photo CD system (explained in Chapter 6) is a new option to conventional photo processing in which the photographer can have film-based images loaded on to a CD for display on the home TV. The photo processing facility will charge a few dollars for the scanning of an image to disc. Investing in a Photo CD drive (about $600) to transfer the CD images to the computer may be a better investment for the digital photographer than a slide scanner, providing that the photographer intends to concentrate on digitizing new images. The Photo CD system, as presently configured and marketed, does not easily accommodate the transfer of older material in different formats.

There will always be a place for digitizers and scanners in the world of digital photography even if or when we reach a point when most new images are recorded on magnetic oxide disks rather than on silver halide

The Newspaper's Role in the Digital Revolution

Much of the early work in digital imaging was shaped by newspaper photography. There were two reasons for this. The newspaper's prepress components were among the first in the printing industry to adopt digital electronics and, as a medium, newspapers have relatively low resolution requirements for reproduction (which made the early technical limitations of digital photography less apparent). As a consequence, much of the digital imaging equipment, as well as the technical standards surrounding it, has been developed with the newspaper market in mind. Amateur photographers wanting to keep current on digital photography should keep one eye on what their colleagues in the newspaper world are up to.

film. In many instances it will be quicker and easier to convert an existing film-based image from a library, book, or picture agency into digital form via a scanner, than to seek out a digital image or to create one. After all, there already exist more than 150 years of traditional photography whose images will have to be integrated into this new medium. Scanners will implement this transition and facilitate the use of hundreds of thousands of classic and historic images in electronic publishing.

6.

Output
and Prepress

Digital photographs exist only as binary numbers inside a computer until they are output, either as an image on a computer monitor or as some form of hardcopy (i.e., a print or transparency). The output mechanism is a critical component of any digital photography system since, regardless of the application, it is usually necessary to reconstruct a visible image from the digital pixel values stored inside the computer. If the application is photo-retouching or color separation, the perceived value of the whole system is often related to how closely the output resembles a conventional photograph.

Digital printers that are capable of producing photographic quality output are one of the most striking technical advances of the computer industry. The first personal computer printers to appear on the market in the early 1980s were able to process and output nothing more than simple text and spreadsheet documents. The first personal computer-based digital photography systems appeared in the mid-1980s using video as their primary output mechanism. Only since 1989 have photographic quality digital printers been available for personal computer systems.

The Proof Is in the Printing

High-quality output from a digital imaging system can be achieved only when both the input device (scanner or camera) and the output device (printer or computer monitor) are capable of processing high-fidelity images. One cannot compensate for a poor-quality scan by using a high-quality printer.

So how does output from a digital photography system compare with a conventional silver halide photographic print? Conventional photography is such a mature technology that most photographers today never need consider the technology of the silver halide process. In contrast, digital photography is still an immature, evolving technology in which the technical quality of the digital print is strongly influenced by the choice of equipment used to produce the print. If money is no object, it is now possible to produce output from a digital photography system that is virtually indistinguishable from a conventionally produced transparency or print. However, since money is almost always an issue, users must decide for themselves the optimal trade-off between equipment cost and technical image quality.

The technical quality of a digital photographic image is measured by its sharpness, definition, contrast, and (if the image is color) color accuracy, just like a conventional photograph. Sharpness definition is determined by the output device's spatial and tonal resolution (see below). Contrast is determined by the output device's tonal or dynamic range. Color accuracy is determined by the complex mathematical representation of color employed by the principal digital photography system components: the scanner, software, and printer.

Resolution. The term "resolution" is often misunderstood and misused in the field of digital photography. There are two distinct components associated with the resolution of a digital photograph: spatial resolution (equivalent to the photographic grain size) and tonal resolution (equivalent to dynamic or tonal range). Both are equally important for the reproduction of a photographic quality digital image.

The spatial resolution of an output device is the easiest to understand since it simply describes how many pixels are needed to fill a square inch of the output device. Since most output devices have the same spatial resolution in the horizontal and vertical directions, spatial resolution is usually measured in "dots per inch" or dpi (or, alternatively, lines per inch) rather than "dots per square inch." In the case of a continuous-tone printer, a "dot" can be thought of as a pixel. The spatial resolution of a digital image printer is thus similar in concept to the silver grain size in a traditional photographic print or transparency; the lower the spatial resolution, the coarser the output image becomes. At a minimum, the output device should be able to render the image pixels at a high enough spatial resolution that the pixels cannot be individually distinguished and thereby disappear into a continuum of color (or monochromatic) tones.

The tonal resolution, on the other hand, is a more complex issue. Digital images must, by definition, divide up the tonal range into a finite number of discrete tonal levels. Digital printers, therefore, cannot render tonal variation as a continuous gradation as can a photograph. If there is an inadequate number of levels to represent the tonal range in the original photograph, there will be a noticeable loss of detail in the shadow, midrange or highlights in the image output. Despite the fact that digital printers are unable to produce continuous tones as output, they are often referred to as continuous-tone printers to distinguish them from halftone printers.

The contrast of a digital photography system's output is determined by the tonal range of the output device. For a color device, this tonal range is often referred to as the device's color gamut. Color gamut is simply a description of the range of colors—from most intense (in terms of brightness and color saturation) to least intense—that the device is capable of producing. For a monochromatic device, this tonal range is simply a measure of the blackest black that the printer can produce (the white point will be set by the paper being used).

Color resolution or grayscale is also usually expressed in terms of the maximum number of color (or tonal) levels per pixel the imaging device is capable of handling. In computer parlance, this is referred to as "bits per pixel." To accurately scan and then reproduce a color negative transparency, a digital imaging system must be capable of handling at least 36 bits per pixel. This translates into 2^{36}, or approximately 68 billion possible color gradations per pixel.

For comparison purposes, the human eye can distinguish fewer than 10 million different shades of color, and a magazine-quality offset printing press can typically reproduce fewer than one million colors. So why is it necessary to process photographic negatives at 36 bits per color? The main reason is to be sure to represent the full tonal range of the negative.

Although most digital photography systems sold in the 1980s had a maximum color resolution of 24 bits per pixel (8 bits each for red, green, and blue), by the end of the decade the industry had started to shift toward 36 bits per pixel on high-end systems (12 pixels per color). This had the obvious advantage of enabling digital photography systems to capture, process, and output images with improved tonal range and tonal resolution. As described above, this move to higher color resolution was especially important for the scanning and digital processing of photographic negatives, which have a higher dynamic range than positive transparencies. Increasingly, in professional applications, especially newspaper photojournalism, as the papers switch to color presses, photographers choose color negative film over transparency film.

Color Accuracy. The second factor affecting the technical quality of an output device is its color accuracy. The color accuracy of a digital photography system describes how good the system is in matching the output of the system to the input. A system with perfect color accuracy would ensure the colors in a scanned print match the colors in the monitor image which, in turn, will match the colors in a digital print output from the system. In practice, this was a problem with most of the first desktop digital photography systems. However, the digital color-matching technology being refined today is expected to solve this problem.

An understanding of the color-matching problem requires an understanding of how digital photography systems represent color information. Desktop color scanners separate a photograph into its red, green and blue (RGB) *primary* or *additive* color components during the scanning process. In fact, the 24-bits-per-pixel color resolution mentioned previously actually consists of 8 bits of red information, 8 bits of green information and 8 bits of blue information. Describing the colors in a digital photograph in terms of its red, green and blue components is referred to as its RGB color.

A "color space" is just a mathematical model used to describe the colors in an image. There are many different possible color spaces, although the two most common are RGB (used for scanners and monitors) and cyan, magenta, yellow (CMY) used for printers. Some color spaces, like hue-saturation-luminance (HSL), are designed to represent color in a way that is similar to the way humans perceive color, and are therefore more intuitive for digital photographers to understand and control. In the HSL color space, hue represents the color itself (e.g., red). Saturation represents the purity of the color (e.g., fire engine red is strongly saturated, rust red is not so saturated). A color with zero saturation becomes a neutral gray. Luminance represents the brightness or intensity of the color.

If a scanned image in the RGB color space representation is to be sent to a computer monitor, it is not necessary to convert the digital image into a different color space representation since computer monitors also work with RGB color signals. The reason that monitors use RGB signals is easy to understand; a monitor with no image displayed on it is black. For an image to be displayed, differing amounts of red, green and blue must be *added* to the display. When maximum amounts of RGB are sent to the screen, white is the result. Hence, the *additive* RGB color space is needed for monitor display.

Even though no color space conversion is necessary to display the image on a monitor, the first problem with color matching can be seen at this point. If the same digital image is displayed on two different RGB monitors, it is likely that the image colors will not match between the two displays. This is due to the fact that RGB is not an absolute measure of color, but is rather a measure of color that is relative to the device on which the image is being displayed (see the section on color calibration later in this chapter). Different monitors will display color differently due to such factors as the phosphors they use and their age.

The color-matching problem is further complicated when the image on the screen must now be transferred to paper. To reproduce a digital image on paper it is necessary to convert the RGB scan image data into the cyan, magenta, yellow and black (which is represented by K, to distinguish it from the blue in RGB color space), CMYK. These secondary or subtractive color components are used by both traditional and digital printers.

The reason that printers require images in CMYK is that a piece of paper with no image printed on it is white. For an image to be printed, differing amounts of red, green, and blue must be *subtracted* from the paper. This is accomplished by adding the secondary (subtractive) colors, cyan, magenta, and yellow. When maximum amounts of CMY are printed on the paper, black is the result (at least in theory—see the section on halftone separation later in this chapter). Hence, the *subtractive* CMY color space is needed for color printing to paper.

The fact that color printing requires RGB image data to be transformed into the CMY color space adds a further complication to the color-matching problem. Like RGB, CMY is only a relative measure of color that depends on the printing press being used, the types of inks employed and many other factors. There is no single optimal formula to translate between RGB and CMY color spaces and the more different types of input and output devices that are introduced into the system, the more complicated the color-matching problem can become.

Output Media

There are three different classes of output media available for digital photographs: computer monitors, digital "hardcopy" printers, and electronic media (e.g., computer disks). These different output paths all have unique properties with which a digital photographer should be familiar.

Computer Monitors. The most common method to output a digital image is to display it on a computer monitor, thereby creating what is called a "soft" proof. Your image is represented on the screen and you can manipulate it, but it remains intangible, just a lot of numbers and electrons floating in its color space. The principal advantage of a computer monitor as an output medium is that it does not use any paper, chemicals, or other consumables. Except for the electricity powering your system, the cost and environmental impact associated with creating a new image on a monitor is insignificant. Of course, before it is either distributed (published) or archived, an image on a monitor must first be transferred onto a more permanent medium (hardcopy or electronic media). While there are now myriad different technologies to accomplish this (see the following sections), one of the cheapest ways is to simply take a photograph of the screen.

Excellent high-resolution color monitors now exist for personal computers that enable photographic quality images to be displayed with startling quality and fidelity. Such monitors have much higher spatial and color resolution than standard TV sets and are correspondingly more expensive. A 13″ high-resolution color monitor (and display card) will typically cost around $1,200 while a high-resolution 19″ color monitor may cost as much as $4,000.

IBM and compatible computer monitors are designed to operate at a fixed image resolution, measured in pixels across, then down, as in 640 (pixels across) by 480 (pixels top to bottom). EGA-compatible monitors (and display cards) are the absolute minimum for acceptable color work. EGA can display 640 by 480 with 16 colors per pixel. EGA monitor/card displays are under $400. VGA has the same 640 by 480 resolution, but with 256 colors per pixel. Super-VGA monitors and cards can display up to 1,024 by 860 with 256 colors per pixel. Super-VGA 15″ monitor/card displays are typically under $800. High-end monitors and cards can display 2,048 by 1,280 (or more) with more than a million colors per pixel, but they can cost well over $4,000. Changing or upgrading to a larger or better monitor usually requires a new card as well.

Most Macintosh monitors are designed to display at 72 dpi, therefore, the bigger the monitor, the more pixels are available for the image. Color cards operate at 8 bits or 24 bits per pixel. This simplifies the selection process, because all you need to decide is whether you need 24-bit color (16 million colors) or can live with 8-bit color (256 colors), then how big a monitor you can afford. Color cards are $400 to $600, and color monitors range from $400 for a 13″ to $2,500 for a 19″ "one-page," and on up from there. You can start small, with a 24-bit card and 13″ monitor, then get a bigger monitor as you can afford it.

The display quality of a computer monitor is a function of its "bandwidth." Bandwidth refers to the amount of "information" that can be transmitted through a particular electronic system and is measured in kHz. In the case of monitors, this amount of information translates directly into image resolution. Factors affecting monitor bandwidth include the monitor's screen size, the maximum screen dots per inch it can display, whether it is interlaced or non-interlaced, and its dot pitch (which is related to dpi).

To minimize cost and transmission bandwidth, standard television sets display images using a technique known as "interlacing." Interlacing is the technique of writing only half of the screen image at a time— every other image line. The screen is written 60 times a second in the U.S. (50 times a second in Europe), so the complete image is rewritten 30 times a second. The phosphors (the light emitters) on the monitor's picture tube normally have a half-life of 1/20th of a second, so the interlaced refresh rate is usually acceptable. A noninterlaced monitor writes the complete image 60 times a second. A consequence of interlacing is that still images tend to flicker slightly. This flicker is rarely noticeable on a TV, since most TV images are in motion, thereby minimizing the perceived flicker. However, this flicker can produce very undesirable image degradation (the phosphors tend to color-shift as they fade) and pronounced eye strain when viewing still images for extended periods, as is the case with a digital photography system. Monitors for digital photography applications should be noninterlaced.

A computer monitor capable of being used in a digital photography system should have at least a 13″ diagonal size (ideally 17″ to 19″), have a spatial resolution of approximately 75 dpi (i.e., 75×75 image pixels will be displayed in one square inch of the monitor), be noninterlaced and have at most a .28mm dot pitch. This translates into about a 30 MHz bandwidth requirement.

In addition to the monitor itself, it will be necessary to buy a video display board to interface the monitor to your computer. It is this video display board that actually defines the color resolution of the displayed image. The display board must contain enough video memory to fill the monitor's screen at whatever color resolution the display board supports (usually 24 bits per pixel for digital photography applications). A typical display board for interfacing a 19″ diagonal color monitor (75 dpi) to a PC will need to be able to store approximately 900 image lines containing 1,024 pixels each. This translates directly into the maximum number of pixels, or largest portion of an image, that can be shown on the monitor. Note, that the digital image itself is likely to be much larger than the available frame memory on the display card. If so, the computer software will automatically shrink (subsample) the digital image to enable a lower spatial resolution version of the image to be displayed on the computer monitor. This does not affect the quality of the image or your ability to work on selected parts of it.

High-resolution color monitors and display boards for Macintosh computers are available from companies such as Apple, E-Machines, Raster-Ops, and Radius. The largest supplier of high-resolution color display boards for IBM PCs and compatibles is TrueVision, Inc., which manufactures the TARGA and NuVista video display boards.

Hardcopy Printers. Of the hundreds of personal computer printers available, the vast majority are designed to reproduce simple text and graphics output. Examples of this type of printer include dot-matrix printers, inkjet, and laser printers. While these printers are usually able to produce excellent results for text and line drawings, they are unable to reproduce the subtle shades and tone variations required for photographic image reproduction. For the digital photographer the digital printers that are capable of reproducing a pleasing quality photographic image in either color or monochrome are relatively few.

Printers that are capable of rendering a photographic image usually produce one of three different types of output media: a reflective print, which, not surprisingly, comes from a device called a printer; a film transparency, which is generated by a slide writer or generator; or a set of four "halftone" color-separation films (used on a traditional printing press), which are the product of film writers or digital imagesetters. Despite their familiar names, they all are printers.

There are two fundamentally different technologies for creating photographic quality prints from digital image data: continuous-tone (or "contone") printing and halftone printing. Both technologies use the three secondary colors, CMY (and sometimes black), to synthesize the large number of different colors needed to print a photographic image. In the case of continuous-tone printers, each pixel in the image is transformed into similar sized overlapping dots of cyan, magenta and yellow ink that are transferred onto the paper at different intensities. The combination of these different intensity dots of ink on top of one another creates the desired color. If you look at a contone print under a loupe you will see a continuous blend of colors rather than the series of dots produced by four-color halftone printing.

One method for halftone printing that entails a two-step fusion of digital and traditional printing technologies is to produce four-color separation films from a digital imagesetter (such as a Linotype L300) and then have the prints produced on a conventional printing press. In this case, the different colors in the print are made up by changing the size of the CMYK ink dots relative to each other, rather than their intensity.

While the traditional halftone process is a two-step process, digital halftone printers can print directly to paper with no intermediary separation film step. However, whereas in traditional halftoning the varying size halftone dots are placed in regular patterns relative to one another (commonly referred to as a "rosette" pattern), digital halftone printers (such as color lasers and inkjet printers) often place the dots in much more complicated (and sometimes random) alignments. This latter process is referred to as "dithering." The dithering process used by many digital color printers can control the size and position of the CMYK halftone ink dot.

Examples of contone printers include thermal dye sublimation printers and film writers, while examples of digital halftone printers include laser, inkjet, and electrophotography printers (see descriptions below). Each of these print technologies has its advantages for particular applications, and there is no single printer technology that can claim to be optimal for all applications.

Choosing a Printer

Depending on the size of your budget and needs, it is now possible to produce prints and transparencies from a digital photography system that are indistinguishable from a conventional photograph. However, such printing devices are still quite expensive, costing between $10,000 and $250,000 and are thus often well beyond the reach of the typical individual user. While choosing a digital photographic printer today is almost always a trade-off between cost and printer performance, tomorrow's printers promise to provide excellent quality results at prices well below $10,000.

The following considerations should be examined before making any purchase of a digital printer. Once you have decided which printer is right for you, find out where a similar model is currently in operation, usually at a service bureau or prepress shop. Then arrange to go there and test it before buying it.

Print Quality. In your evaluation process, the primary considerations in evaluating technical print quality are the printer's spatial and tonal resolution, its dynamic range and its color accuracy. Digital printer quality ranges from the barely acceptable (for the most inexpensive printers), to a level that is almost indistinguishable from a photographic original. To approach photographic quality, reflective art printers, that is, machines that produce flat art like a standard office copier, must be capable of printing images with at least 16-bits-per-pixel color resolution and 200 dpi spatial resolution. In general, the higher the quality, the higher the price.

Output Media. Most digital printers allow output to only one kind of media (e.g., paper or film). However, some printers, in particular inkjet printers, can print onto a wide variety of different substrate materials. While the primary consideration in choosing the best output media is the intended application, output to photographic film probably provides the photographer with the most convenient path between the world of conventional photography and photographic printing. Having your final image as a 35mm slide will enable it to be used in the widest variety of applications, at least for the foreseeable future.

Maximum Print Size. The required maximum print size will obviously depend on your application. Digital transparency printers are available for producing anything from a 35mm slide up to a $10'' \times 12''$ chrome. Digital reflective art printers are available for producing anything from a postcard sized print up to a large poster. Most digital printers are limited to producing only one size of output, however.

Cost of the Printer. Prices of photographic quality digital printers range from under $10,000 to over $200,000. At the low end of this range, it is possible to buy a reasonable quality 35mm film recorder or $4'' \times 5''$ thermal dye sublimation printer for around $10,000. (These are described in detail below.)

Cost per Copy. Even after a printer is purchased there is still a finite cost associated with the consumables (mainly the paper, film and/or ink) used in generating the print. This cost per copy can range from as little as 15 cents a print for plain paper color copiers to as much as $15 a print for large format thermal dye sublimation printers. Of course, if the printer is a film recorder, the cost per copy is the expense of the film and processing. In addition, the printer maintenance costs should be factored into this cost per copy consideration, as it would with any hardware purchase.

Software and Computer Compatibility. Once you have selected the printer that is right for your application, make sure that it can be attached to the personal computer that you intend to use. This sounds elementary, but system integration is a complicated, and in some cases impossible task. Make sure that you have the correct cables to link your printer and computer. In addition, it is important to establish whether the electronic imaging software that you intend to use contains a software printer driver designed to work with your intended printer. Not every printer can be attached to every personal computer system and not all image-processing software can output images to every printer.

Processing Speed. Precisely placing the thousands of discrete dots of color on paper or film takes time. If your primary emphasis is on output quality, the fact that it may take several minutes to produce a single print may not concern you. However, if you intend to use the printer for short-run print production, then the time it takes to execute a hard copy of the image, called "throughput," will be a primary consideration. Some copier printers take a number of minutes to produce the first print after which subsequent copies are produced at a much faster rate.

Fade Resistance. Digital printer vendors are often reluctant to talk about the fade resistance (or permanence) of the output that their printer produces. However, as every professional photographer knows, even film dyes will fade over time. If you intend to archive your digital prints for a number of years, try to find out the fade characteristics of the print technology you are interested in. For example, some thermal dye sublimation prints have been observed to fade dramatically in just a few months. Obtaining information on the fade characteristics of digital printers can be extremely difficult, since, in many cases, the printer manufacturers themselves haven't measured the fade characteristics of their printer dye. Companies that have taken the time and have the know-how to understand the fade characteristics of their digital printers are the traditional photography and chemical companies (i.e., Kodak, Fuji, DuPont, etc.) that are now producing digital photography peripherals. If you buy a printer from one of these companies, you can probably get all the information on fade characteristics you need directly from the manufacturer.

Of course, for total resistance to any aging effects, the best solution is to archive the image in digital format. With the cost of storage media declining all the time, most prudent photographers store digital back-up copies of their images on disk or tape.

Reflective Art Printers (Paper Printers)

Photographers are more accustomed to seeing their work on paper or film but digital imaging technology is increasing the options. Likewise, printers can, as we've seen, output to hard copy other than paper. Because of this, the industry tends to call these devices by the more accurate (but more ponderous) term "reflective art printers." For the purposes of this book, and unless otherwise stated, when we say a printer we mean a device that outputs reflective art—in most instances, a paper print. Numerous competing technologies are available for producing prints from a digital photograph and each technology has its own intrinsic strengths and weaknesses depending on the application.

The principal technologies for producing photographic-quality reflective art prints from a digital photography system fall into the following categories:

Inkjet Printers. Inkjet printers work by shooting different sized small drops of ink onto the paper surface. As with a conventional printing press, an inkjet printer typically uses the four basic printing ink colors—cyan, magenta, yellow, and black—to create a color image. However, unlike a printing press, these images are typically created through a process of "dithering" rather than halftone screening.

Because of the basic similarity between the way inkjet printers and traditional printing presses create images (spots of ink on paper), the maximum quality level of an inkjet printer resembles the quality of a four-color offset printing press. For this reason inkjet printers are good candidates for producing prepress image proofs. Like printing presses, however, inkjet printers are not capable of producing truly "photographic quality" prints due to the limited tonal range that is achievable by the deposition of four colors of ink onto paper.

Companies manufacturing inkjet printers include Iris Graphics (a subsidiary of Scitex) and Hewlett-Packard. The Iris printer is capable of producing large-format prints of remarkable quality on almost any substrate material.

The principal advantages of inkjet printer technology are its low cost per print and its relatively high quality. The low cost per print results from the low cost of the consumables used in creating the print (plain paper and liquid ink). The relatively high print quality results from the high spatial resolution that is possible when depositing ink onto paper in such small increments (drop sizes). Another advantage of some inkjet printers is their ability to produce very large format output onto a variety of different papers, such as plain, silk, or even rice paper.

There are, however, a couple of disadvantages to inkjet printers. Since inkjet printers that are capable of producing high-quality output require very precise mechanisms for controlling the flow of ink onto the paper, they can be quite expensive (as much as $75,000 in the case of the

Iris printer). Another disadvantage of inkjet printing technology is the agonizingly long time some inkjet printers require to produce a print.

Thermal Dye Sublimation. Thermal dye sublimation technology is an example of a continuous-tone printer (see description above). Thermal dye sublimation printers contain a roll of inked ribbon that contains the dye pigments used in the printing. This material is in contact with a strip of thousands of small heating elements contained in the print head. As each row of pixels in the digital image is sent to the printer, each element in the strip is heated proportionately to the intensity of the color in the corresponding pixel. This heating process causes the dye pigments to be sublimated into a gaseous form. The hotter the print head element, the more dye is sublimated. The sublimation process causes a slight spreading and melding of color that results in thousands of shades of near continuous-tone images.

Thermal dye sublimation printers are available from companies such as Kodak, DuPont, Nikon and Sony. Thermal dye sublimation printers capable of producing small format prints (approximately 4″ × 5″) are available for under $5,000, while large format printers that can produce output up to 10″ × 12″ cost between $15,000 and $40,000. Most thermal dye sublimation printers use a three-color process (CMY) to produce the continuous-tone prints. The DuPont 4-Caster printer uses a fourth color (black) in the printing process in addition to the always needed CMY colors. Using a solid black ink instead of a mixture of the cyan, magenta, and yellow inks tends to produce better-looking blacks (and hence better tonal range) because impurities in the CMY inks make it difficult to create a good three-color black. Four-color thermal dye sublimation printers are more expensive, however, due to the greater complexity of the printer design.

The advantages of thermal dye printers are that they are relatively inexpensive (especially if you only need the smaller sized output), fairly fast, and the print quality approaches photographic quality. In fact, the dynamic range and theoretical spatial resolution limits on thermal dye sublimation technology exceed that of silver halide prints. The technology's main drawback is that the printer requires special paper that is quite expensive (approximately $1 a print for the small format, and $10 per print for the larger format).

The digital printers marketed for printing still video images (so-called still video printers) are all based on thermal dye sublimation technology. Because some of these printers were initially marketed for video printing applications they may not support a digital computer interface. Although such printers can still be attached to a personal computer through a video frame-grabber device, some quality is lost in this process and a direct digital connection is preferable.

Electrophotography. Electrophotography is the technology behind standard office photocopiers and laser printers. In the case of a photocopier, an electrostatic charge is created on a drum by projecting onto it an optical image of the object to be copied. This electrostatic charge attracts toner that is then transferred to the paper. In the case of a laser printer, the electrostatic charge is created by a laser instead of the optical projection system. Although most laser printers are black-and-white devices, color laser printers are now available for under $4,000. Color electrophotographic printing is a halftone process.

In place of the single-color (usually black) toner fluid used in standard office copiers and laser printers, color electrostatic printers and copiers usually employ four-color CMYK dry powder inks. Due to a number of factors, including the different image-forming characteristics of dry toner versus liquid ink, the maximum achievable quality level of color copiers and electrostatic printers is somewhat inferior to that of an offset press or high-quality inkjet printer.

Full-color photocopiers are now available from a number of vendors. A number of these color photocopiers are available with optional digital (computer) interfaces, effectively turning them into short-run color printers. The distinctions between digital color printers, color photocopiers and, eventually, color fax machines, will continue to blur. Digital color copiers are optimized for the rapid reproduction of color graphics and text. High-quality reproduction of digital images is often a secondary consideration for these devices.

The most successful color copier on the market today is the Canon CLC-500. It is capable of producing color copies (or prints from a computer) of remarkable quality at the rate of about 15 copies a minute. The Canon CLC-500 is based on electrophotographic imaging technology and is capable of rendering high-quality color copies. With the addition of a Canon-supplied digital interface accessory, the copier can be turned into a short-run digital printer.

The Canon CLC-500 is capable of printing onto plain paper and the resulting low cost per copy, and the printer's relatively high speed, make it ideal for short-run printing applications. The printer is being rapidly adopted by service bureaus (see below) to support short-run color printing for color desktop publishing applications.

Despite the fact that the CLC-500 is still too expensive for personal use (approximately $60,000 when configured as a digital printer), color electrophotographic printing technology has no major disadvantages and could become the first mass produced (i.e., low cost) high-quality digital proofing printer.

Other manufacturers with plain paper copiers include Kodak, Savin and Brother. Fuji has introduced a copier, called the Color Copier AP5000, that is really a self-contained photochemical print enlarger and duplicator positioned as a color photocopier. It is not clear whether devices of this type belong in a one-hour photo shop or a photocopy service bureau. Ilford recently introduced its Cibacopy system that is a color copier capable of producing high-quality, large-format transparencies as output.

Of the commonly available reflective printers, thermal dye sublimation printers may provide the best cost performance for digital photography applications. Thermal dye sublimation printers are relatively low cost and are capable of producing prints that can accurately be described as near-photographic quality. Electrostatic copiers and printers are most useful as short-run printers for desktop publishing applications, while inkjet printers are most useful for prepress proofing and large-format printing applications.

Over the next few years there are likely to be other digital color printer technologies reaching the market. Despite the fact that many will offer significant advantages over traditional silver halide photography in terms of speed and convenience, all will ultimately be evaluated on the basis of how closely they can match the extraordinarily high quality and low cost per copy associated with film.

Film Writers

Film writers are, as the name suggests, digital printers that produce photographic transparencies as their final output. In other words, a digital image is fed into the device and an exposed roll of slide film comes out. The spatial and color resolution of many of today's film writers is good enough to produce transparencies that are difficult to distinguish from a photographically derived original. The majority of desktop film writers produce 35mm slides, whereas the higher end film writers produce transparencies of sizes $4'' \times 5''$ and larger.

Most film writers contain some form of modified film camera body pointed at a cathode ray tube (CRT) display screen. The camera shutter remains open while the red, green, and blue electron beams inside the CRT sweep across the face of the tube exposing the film. The intensity of the RGB electron beam at each position on the CRT is a function of the image pixel value at that position. Each line of the image causes the CRT to illuminate the face of the CRT and expose the film at that location. Once the whole image has been "written," line by line, to the CRT display, the exposed film is removed from the camera and developed in the normal way.

The cost for 35mm film writers is typically under $10,000 and they are available from a number of companies, including Agfa, Matrix and Polaroid. They are usually capable of imaging up to 8,000 lines of image data onto a 35mm slide (i.e., a spatial resolution of approximately 5,800 lines per inch!). For comparison purposes, the grain size of a typical ASA 200 slide film is about 3,000 grains per inch. Any 35mm film can be used with these film writers, and Polachrome instant 35mm slide film can be used if instant output is required.

Film writers capable of producing $4'' \times 5''$ transparencies typically cost from $15,000 to $35,000, and can support resolutions up to 16,000 lines per inch. Larger format film writers ($8''$ x $10''$ and above) can cost well over $200,000 and are typically found only in professional prepress and state-of-the-art electronic photo studios.

One of the biggest challenges facing the use of film writers in digital photography applications is color matching, or color calibration (see below). Electronic-imaging technology has not yet made it easy to produce digital transparencies that precisely match the scanned original. Once this has been accomplished, slide writers will be used for producing second-generation originals and high-quality internegatives from digital image scans.

Halftone Separation Film Writers

If your digital image is to be used in a publication or document that will be printed on a traditional four-color printing press, it, like a traditional photograph, will have to be converted into four separation negatives. It is now possible to produce high-quality color separations from your personal computer with most image-processing software. It is unlikely, however, that most photographers will go to the trouble of generating such film, but will leave that function to a prepress house or service bureau. This function is typically a cost accrued by the publisher of the image. However, if a photographer decides to be his or her own publisher for a book or promotional mailing, for example, some savings may be had by the photographer making his or her own color separation negatives.

Color separation for printing consists of two steps. Since a traditional printing press uses four colors—cyan, magenta, yellow, and black (CMYK)—to reproduce a photograph, the photograph must first be broken down or "separated" into its CMYK components. A separate image file is generated representing the tonal values of each of the CMYK components needed to reproduce the photograph at each spatial position in the image. At the same time, these CMYK tonal values must be broken down into a series of differing size dots by a process known as "screening." The size of the dots in the screen varies according to the type of press and paper being used. The final result is four black-and-white transparencies (usually negatives) called "halftones."

This screening process is necessary because the four colors of ink cannot actually be printed on top of each other to produce the desired final color. Instead, the tiny dots of CMYK inks are placed in small tightly grouped circular patterns known as rosettes. From a normal reading distance, these dot patterns are invisible and the image appears to be continuous. The color separation process is best understood by looking at any printed "four-color" picture through a magnifying glass (or loupe). Whereas, to the naked eye the picture looks like a photograph, through the magnifying glass you will see the myriad CMYK dots of different sizes in regular patterns.

The traditional process for making halftone separations involved exposing film through a series of color filters and a fine mesh screen. This method has now been replaced by a process involving computers, software, and electronic scanners.

Unlike the high-end drum scanners used by the professional prepress houses, which can scan and convert a photograph directly into its CMYK (analog) components, desktop scanners produce red, green and blue (RGB) color files from the scanned photograph. Therefore, once photo-retouching software has been used to manipulate this RGB image into the desired size and appearance for printing, it must next be color separated into its CMYK color components for printing.

The conversion from RGB to CMY color space is simple in theory. Since the CMY colors are the complement colors to RGB colors, it should be possible to simply "invert" the RGB pixel values to create the corresponding CMY values. In fact, in order to produce good-looking printed images, the conversion formula is enormously more complicated than this.

Of course, it has been possible to do electronic color separation on high-end prepress systems from vendors such as Scitex, Crossfield, Hell Graphics and Dai Nippon Screen since the early 1980s. However, up until very recently, these were largely "closed" systems in which the scanning, retouching and separation film writing were all performed on the same system and connectivity with personal computer systems was considered to be neither necessary nor possible.

Since 1988 the increasing quality and convenience of desktop color software and peripherals has both pushed the prepress system vendors to provide connectivity solutions with the desktop and caused the desktop publishing vendors to incorporate color imaging and separation technology into their products. Color separation is, however, a very complex process, embodying a closely held trade art that has evolved over many years. The last few years have therefore seen a mad scramble to incorporate this knowledge into personal computer software. One of the main challenges in this process has been to translate the terms and controls used by professionals (e.g., "Under Color Removal" and "Gray Component Replacement") into controls that are more intuitive to the amateur user.

The process of doing a color separation from a personal computer–based system is fairly straightforward. First the RGB scanned image file must be color balanced, sized and, if necessary, retouched using whatever photo-retouching software is being used (see Chapter 4). This RGB file must then be input to a color separation program (sometimes the same as the photo-retouching software). This color separation software allows the user to customize the color separation process for the characteristics of the particular printing press, inks and paper stock that will be used in the printing process.

The output of the color separation program depends on the type of hardware that will be used to produce the halftone films themselves. If the halftone films are to be produced on a high-end prepress system (e.g., a Scitex system) the CMYK separations can be output in the Scitex-CT (for "continuous tone") format. In this case the screening process is performed on the high-end system's drum scanner. A Scitex-CT file can be transferred from a desktop personal computer to a Scitex system via, for example, the Scitex Gateway using a Macintosh-based Scitex Visionary system.

An alternative to producing the separation films on a high-end system is to use a PostScript-compatible digital imagesetter such as the Linotype L300. If the intent is to use a digital imagesetter like the L300, the separation software must produce the four CMYK separation files in the PostScript (or "encapsulated PostScript") format. These files are then sent to the digital imagesetter for outputting to film. Once the separation films have been produced they can be used to create a match print (e.g., a Chromalin) or sent to the printer in the normal fashion.

The Linotype L300 has a dot resolution of approximately 2,500 dpi and is able to produce halftone dots with 256 levels of gray at a maximum resolution of approximately 150 line screen. In theory, this is adequate for almost all printing applications, since there are very few printing presses in the world that can deliver a print resolution higher than this. In practice, however, even though the quality of desktop color separations has increased dramatically over the past few years, digital imagesetters cannot yet consistently match the quality and throughput of high end prepress systems. However, we are very close to the time when digital imagesetters and desktop color separation systems will produce results of comparable quality to today's million dollar prepress systems.

Before embarking down the path of do-it-yourself color separations, it is important to consider whether it is sensible to attempt this stage of the process from your desktop system. Color separation is more a part of the image production cycle than it is a part of the photographic creative cycle. The photographer has traditionally been far removed from this process, since it has been the job of the prepress production house to control the separation parameters and take responsibility for the quality of the final separation. The desktop computer, however, gives the photographer an opportunity to recapture much of the artistic control over his or her work that has been lost to the prepress system retoucher. In addition, the cost savings associated with using a desktop system for color separation work must be carefully analyzed. The biggest cost savings in doing color separation on a personal computer comes not from color separating a single image, but from electronically "stripping" (assembling) a complex page before it is sent to the printers.

Output to Electronic Media

A traditional photograph provides both a display and storage for the image. These functions are often separated in a digital photography system. A monitor, for example, can display an image but not store it, while a computer disk can store a digital image but not display it. A computer disk is, in fact, the most common form of output in a digital photography system, because having it only on a TV screen is not a concept that the traditional photographer finds especially convenient.

For many applications, using a disk to store a digital photograph is more cumbersome than a traditional photographic image, because a separate display device is required. A significant advantage of the electronic storage of digital images, however, is its resistance to aging effects. Unlike almost any type of color hardcopy media (photographic or otherwise), a digital image stored on a disk (especially on a medium known as a magneto optical disk) in a safe place will remain unchanged for a very long time (although deteriorization has been observed over a 10-year period).

Electronic media suitable for storing or archiving digital images includes magnetic disks and digital tape systems (e.g., DAT) and magneto optical disks. Even VCR tapes can be used for storing huge amounts of digital data. In addition, Kodak's Photo CD system will make it practical to archive photographs onto CD-ROM discs that can be played back on your TV or loaded into your personal computer system. Photographers will be able to bring their exposed film into a photo-processing store and, instead of being processed as prints or slides, the images will be returned to them on a compact disc (CD) that looks very similar to today's audio compact disc. These discs will be compatible with Photo CD players (available from Philips and others) that will allow the photographer to view the images on a standard TV set. Indubitably, Photo CD systems will be introduced that incorporate features for electronic color correction, cropping, and retouching. Thus the Photo CD system may be the catalyst for the first mass market electronic photography darkroom.

Photo CD is a hybrid digital photography system, using traditional film cameras to capture the image and electronic devices to output it. In this sense, Photo CD represents a stepping stone in the process from traditional photographic systems using silver halide processing, to the all-digital "filmless" cameras of the future. Eventually, digital cameras will be able to write the images directly to a compact disc within the camera itself.

Service Bureaus

As discussed earlier, photographic quality digital color printers may be an impractical expense for the average photographer. Fortunately for such individuals, there is an increasing number of "service bureaus" around the country that lease access time to such equipment. In some instances the photographer may be allowed to operate the equipment, or the bureau's technician will perform the services under the photographer's supervision or to his or her specification.

Many of today's computerized service bureaus are a direct outgrowth of photocopy ("quick copy") shops. The typical computerized service bureaus will own a number of personal computers (usually Macintoshes, with some IBMs or compatibles) attached to a variety of laser printers and digital typesetters. Service bureaus predate desktop color imaging technology and are an outgrowth of the desktop publishing revolution.

Today's more advanced service bureaus provide access to desktop color scanners and color printers and can even support on-site color separations using a PostScript-compatible digital typesetter. In addition, many service bureaus now have color photocopiers that, when used in conjunction with a digital interface attachment, can provide a short-run printing and proofing service to the digital photographer.

As service bureaus increasingly adopt color technology, the distinction between a "photocopy style" computerized service bureau and a one-hour photo lab will start to diminish. This blurring will be increased as the photo labs start to adopt electronic imaging technology, such as Kodak's Photo CD system.

Color Calibration

Maintaining color fidelity and accuracy (color matching) between the input and output is one of the most important and yet elusive aspects of any digital photography system. While one of the allures of digital photography is the ability to create almost unlimited special effects, most desktop systems are, at the present time, unable to perform the most fundamental task of all—scanning an original print or transparency and producing a copy that matches precisely the original. Likewise, a color image on a computer monitor will not necessarily print out with the same color values. These problems are the result of inadequate color calibration in most desktop digital photography systems.

Prior to the advent of desktop photography systems and peripherals, color calibration was not really a problem. This was due to the fact that color electronic imaging systems (mostly in use in the prepress industry) were large, self-contained systems costing upwards of $1 million. However, with the advent of inexpensive desktop systems, it has become necessary to support a vast array of different color-imaging peripherals, each one with a different set of color-matching characteristics. This has given rise to a need for a standard mechanism to describe color image data for the purpose of exchanging it between different color peripherals.

The color calibration problem, while easy to describe, is not so easy to solve. The most commonly used "device independent" measure of color in use by the electronic imaging industry today is based on a standard known as the CIE color space. This standard is at the center of almost all of today's efforts to define a universal digital interchange standard for communicating color information. Once a CIE-based color standard has been universally adopted, all scanners, cameras, monitors and printers will need to be characterized in terms of this device independent color space.

The Future of Output

Over the next few years we can look forward to a proliferation of inexpensive photographic quality digital printers. These printers will eventually meet, and in many cases exceed, the sharpness definition and color accuracy of silver halide film. Standards will soon be defined for the representation and calibration of the color information in digital photographs. These standards will allow electronic images to be effortlessly transferred across multiple locations, devices, and media with no change in color appearance.

Digital photography promises to revolutionize the way we think about photographic output. Traditional photography requires that we produce the "output" (developed film or print) before we can decide if we like the picture and want to keep it. Digital photography will allow us to preview images on a monitor (and possibly alter them electronically) before we decide whether to make a print. This reduction in the cost of consumables will set photographers free to experiment more freely than ever before with the creative process of taking a photograph.

7.

Transmission: Moving Digital Images around the World

One of the most exciting aspects of digital photography is the ability to send and receive digitized photographic images over conventional telephone lines. Whether it's sending a family snapshot to a relative or a stock picture to a potential client, photographs can be at the recipient's residence in minutes instead of days, provided that the sender and receiver have a computer and an attached modem.

Even now, photojournalists can take an electronic photograph of a late-breaking news event and transmit the image back to their newspaper's photo desk by telephone in time to meet a deadline only minutes away. The transmission of digital photographs direct from photographers in the field to their publications gives the newspaper or magazine an exclusive as well as an alternative to the heavily used wire service photos. Digital photo transmission is also expected to play an integral role in the marketing of images to advertising agencies and graphic design firms.

Compared to television, which sends literally millions of images over the airwaves daily to millions of receivers already installed in the home, sending a single scanned photograph across a phone line by computer may seem unimpressive and needlessly complicated. But if you were ever able to grab a single televised image, freeze it and transfer it to paper, you would be surprised at how crude a TV image is when compared to a still photograph. That's because even the average snapshot made with today's point-and-shoot 35mm camera will yield a color image with much more detail and color than that found in a single still image from a network broadcast. Still photographs are significantly more detailed and complex than TV images and, as such, take more time and effort to transmit electronically.

Surprisingly, you don't have to have the array of expensive equipment required for TV transmission to send an image electronically. In fact, the most significant breakthrough is the price of the equipment necessary to electronically transmit still images. It is now possible for high-resolution digital photographs to be transmitted across the world through a normal telephone line with equipment costing less than $5,000.

Once a photographic image has been converted into electronic form—and not just into a digital form but to an analog video signal also—it can be transmitted through any medium used for transmitting electronic signals. For example, it can be transmitted via cable or satellite in the same way that TV signals are transmitted. Alternatively, it can be transmitted via the airwaves like a traditional radio or television signal. However, the most accessible and cheapest medium for image transmission is the standard telephone line.

Any personal computer equipped with a modem (see below) is capable of sending and receiving digital files over telephone lines. Until recently, modems have most effectively been used for sending text. When color graphics or photographic images needed to be transmitted, problems arose due to the larger amount of data required to represent a color image.

For comparison purposes, a single page of typed text contains about 2,500 bytes (or 20,000 bits) of data. Using a high-speed 9,600 baud modem, it would take approximately 2 seconds to transmit the full page across a phone line. By comparison, a digitized 35mm color slide contains about 15 megabytes of data (depending on the resolution of the scan). This file would take about 3.5 hours to transmit.

Obviously, this would be too long to wait, and too costly in phone bills and man-hours, so an alternative approach had to be found. One way that would be faster would be to use a more efficient transmission medium, such as fiber optic cable, or use a satellite that has a wider "bandwidth" (for more data throughput). Few have access to such technology, so another alternative was developed, a software solution that would "compress" the size of the digital image file prior to phone line transmission.

Compression algorithms were developed that reduced all the numbers in the image file to more efficient equations representing the whole image file. Thus, the compressed images would be packaged for more convenient transfer and then, once received, "decompressed" to their original size so that they could be displayed and printed. The technique is not unlike the manufacture of orange juice that is condensed for shipping at a plant and reconstituted at home.

One of the most ubiquitous "image" transmission systems to take advantage of data compression is the fax machine. In contrast to the digital image transmission systems, the fax machine does not (currently) need to transmit color images. Instead, it must send a full-page black-and-white two-tone image over the phone line in just a few seconds. The fax machine digitizes each page (containing text, graphics and images) at a resolution of 200 dpi. Thus for an $8.5'' \times 11''$ page, the fax machine must send 3,740,000 bits of data.

Using the 9,600 baud modem contained in most modern fax machines, the transmission time would be 6.5 minutes. Of course, anyone who has used a fax machine knows that it doesn't take 6.5 minutes to send a single page—on average a single page can be transmitted in 15 seconds, or 25 times as fast. The fax machine accomplishes this by using internal image compression hardware to compress the data file. At the other end, the receiving fax machine reverses this process by decompressing the file so that it can be printed out with no apparent loss of information. So what is going on here?

Image compression, whether for black-and-white fax images or for full-color digital photographs, is typically used to reduce the size of images to allow more of them to be stored on a disk, or to increase the speed at which an image can be electronically transmitted through a given medium (e.g., across a phone line).

Just as reconstituted orange juice will not be identical to fresh-squeezed, compressed images are different from the original. The objective is always to remove only that information from the image that can be reconstructed at the receiving end with no noticeable degradation. There are two ways that this is done, each requiring certain compromises, however.

Most image compression techniques involve some loss of image fidelity, although the loss is not considered crucial for most purposes. There are some techniques, however, that do not cause any loss of information when the image is decompressed. This type of image compression technique is known as lossless or non-destructive compression. (The converse is lossy or destructive compression.) An image that has been compressed using a lossless compression technique can be decompressed into an exact replica of the original image prior to compression. The principal disadvantage of this approach is that lossless image compression techniques only reduce the file size (and, correspondingly, the transmission time) of a digitized photograph by about 50 percent.

Any compression technique that is to be really useful for the transmission of digitized photographs must reduce the amount of data needed to represent the image by at least 90 percent. There are numerous techniques that can accomplish this, but all involve some amount of non-reversible data loss. These techniques attempt to discard image information that the human eye is least likely to notice as missing. For example, the eye is more sensitive to certain spatial frequencies than it is to others. By taking advantage of the psychophysics of human perception, reductions in image data size can be effected with little noticeable degradation.

A sophisticated image compression technique known as the Adaptive Discrete Cosine Transform (ADCT) has been developed that involves very little noticeable loss of image fidelity, even when used with compression ratios as high as 30:1. ADCT has been endorsed and is being promoted as a standard for adoption by the Joint Photographic Experts Group (JPEG), an industry trade organization. It is expected that ADCT will become the standard that will allow image transmission hardware and software from a variety of manufacturers to exchange compressed image files with little difficulty and greater fidelity.

Image Transmission Equipment

There are basically two different types of image transmission systems: A "stand-alone" image transceiver device and a computer-based image transceiver. The choice between these two depends on the application.

Stand-Alone Image Transceivers. Stand-alone image transceivers contain all the necessary hardware and software components for image transmission within a single unit that is about the size of a stereo receiver. There are two different types of stand-alone image transceiver equipment—photographic image transceivers and still video image transceivers.

Photographic image transceivers are designed to enable the user to transmit (or receive) a digital image that is the equivalent of a 35mm transparency (either positive or negative) of that image over a standard telephone line. These transceivers are not able to transmit prints. This type of image transceiver contains a 35mm film scanner that takes the developed film image and turns it into a digital file, the image compression technology that makes it easy to transport, and a high-speed modem to send it on its way—all within a single box. The power supply may be either 110 volts AC or 12 volts DC depending on whether the unit has been designed for fixed-base or field use.

The best-known example of this type of photographic image transmitter is the Leafax 35, made by Leaf Systems of Natick, Massachusetts. Leaf was a little-known company in the medical imaging business before being awarded a contract from the Associated Press to develop a portable digital image transceiver. Shortly thereafter Leaf was designated the primary technology supplier to the AP, which is a cooperative owned by 950 newspapers in the U.S. As a result, the Leafax 35 and its successor products became the *de facto* standard in the American newspaper market. Similar systems exist from different manufacturers that include Nikon, Sinclair, and Hasselblad, which are better represented in Europe and the Pacific Rim. All transmit in analog or digital mode but digital transmission will eventually be the predominant mode. The cost of these transceivers ranges from $15,000 to $50,000 depending on options.

Still video transceivers are designed to enable the user to transmit (or receive) a single-frame video image over a standard telephone line. This type of image transceiver contains a video frame grabber (for digitizing and displaying a color video image), image compression technology, and a high-speed modem. Manufacturers of still video image transceivers include Sony, Kodak, Canon, and Nikon. The cost of these transceivers ranges from $12,000 to $30,000.

Personal Computer–Based Systems. An alternative to the stand-alone image transceiver is a properly equipped personal computer. It is possible to turn a personal computer into a high-resolution image transceiver system with the addition of about $1,000 to $2,000 of hardware and software.

While there is some flexibility in the configuration of a home computer for image transmission, the minimum addition is a modem and its associated telecommunication software. A modem (**mo**dulator/**dem**odulator) is a hardware device that, once attached to the system between the phone line and the computer, enables the computer to send and receive digital data files over any phone line.

The most important feature of a modem is its speed (often measured in baud or bits per second). Modem speeds range from a low of 300 baud (less than $100) to the blindingly fast 19,200-bit-per-second modems ($500 to $1,000). In the future modem speed will likely increase to 64K Baud with the advent of ISDN telephone lines. Since digital photographs tend to be very large, the faster the modem, the better for sending images. In purchasing a modem, however, make sure that whatever model you choose is compatible with the software that you plan to use it with. Perhaps the most common types of modem for use with personal computers (Macs and PCs) are Hayes-compatible modems. Most software supports the Hayes standard.

Using a high-speed modem will help reduce the image transmission time, but not to an acceptable time duration for the average professional photographer who is likely to want to send high-quality images (and therefore large image files). Image compression must still be employed. (It should be noted that some high-speed modems use their own internal compression which, when applied to an already compressed image, may actually cause the file to expand and thus slow the transmission down. These internal compression schemes should be disabled, or these devices avoided if one is transmitting a compressed image.)

Image compression is accomplished by either a software program installed on the computer's hard disk or by a hardware add-on product (usually a plug-in board installed inside the computer). Image compression is a mathematically complex procedure that can take up a lot of processing time with the average personal computer. For this reason, hardware accelerator devices, which are cards or boards installed inside the computer, are often used to shorten the time required to compress an image. The accelerator board functions much like a turbocharger on an engine—it speeds up the processing time of complex calculations like compression algorithms. Image compression hardware and software is available from a variety of vendors for both the Mac and the PC. The software retails for under $200; the hardware for under $1,000.

Selecting the Right System. Image transceiver systems based on personal computers are large, heavy instruments and space intensive, but cost-effective if you already own a personal computer and a scanner. Stand-alone image transceivers are smaller, have smaller power requirements and travel better. Some are specifically made as mobile units and are extremely compact, fitting in a specially designed container the size of a "one-suiter" suitcase. These units are one-way, however, designed for the photographer in the field who only needs to send an image.

The Future of Transmission

Future image transceivers will be smaller and more portable. Sony has already introduced a 12-volt DC still video transceiver that can be installed in a car. In the more distant future, electronic cameras will contain built-in transceivers, allowing the camera to be plugged directly into the phone line for instant image transmission. Portable satellite dishes, which fit in a small case, will provide instant "uplinks" with orbiting communication satellites. Using these new technologies, freelance photographers will be able to compete directly with wire services and not even have to compete for an available phone line.

Stock photography houses, as well as individual photographers with large photographic collections, will archive their transparencies as digital images in computerized image databases. If these databases are connected to a telecommunications device, potential buyers of images will be able to electronically—and remotely—search through stock photo databases by typing key word descriptors of the images. Once a desired photograph is located, the digital image file will be sent electronically, along with the invoice for usage.

Part Two

The Results

8.

Digital Gallery

Digital technologies will change the way that photographers depict the world, just as has every other technical development in photography, from the view camera to the 35mm SLR, and from the daguerreotype to T-MAX film. The images included here by a number of photographers using some of the early digital imaging technology, suggest what the merger of the computer and the camera will bring.

The technical processes that produced these images vary, as noted in the captions with each image. Many of the images could have been made using traditional photographic methods, although it would have taken more time and, in some cases, expense. A few of the images show that the computer is much more than another kind of darkroom. It is a device that not only enhances but extends the range of human perception.

What makes a successful digital photograph? It's easy to say what it takes technically: resolution, color fidelity, and an absence of artifacts. In time, the origin of digital photographs won't be an issue any more than it is in any other creative medium. The gallery of pioneering work that follows hints at the fact that the only limits of digital imaging are the creators' imaginations.

"Portrait of Neil Young." *Graham Nash, the pop musician-turned-photographer, enhanced this portrait of his former singing partner Neil Young using digital image processing tools.*

"Tom." *Peter Voci's "synthetic
portrait" uses image
processing to superimpose a
face over a skull as part of a
demonstration in
forensic pathology.*
"Serenity of Flight."
*Lawrence Gartel uses digital
imagery to create photographic
illustrations such as this cover
picture for* Forbes.

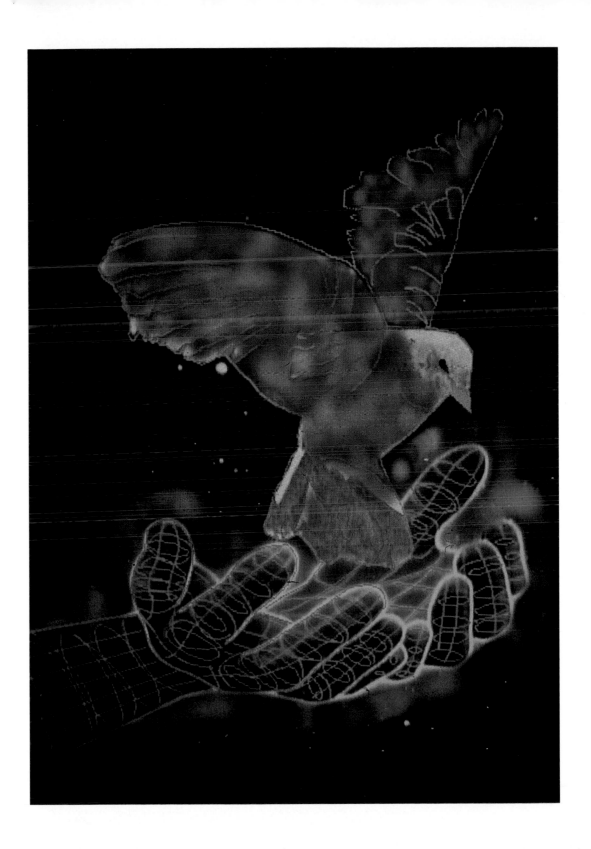

"The Ecstasy of Ludovica Albertoni." *Paul Solomon's nude study was manipulated with Adobe Photoshop software. Creative direction and photography by Paul Solomon © 1991. Makeup by Rochelle Weithorn.*
"Tikis." *David Brunn proves that black-and-white can be a powerful medium in the color-dominated world of digital photography.*

"Searching for Piranesi." Terry Gips, a University of Maryland art instructor, created this electronic image.

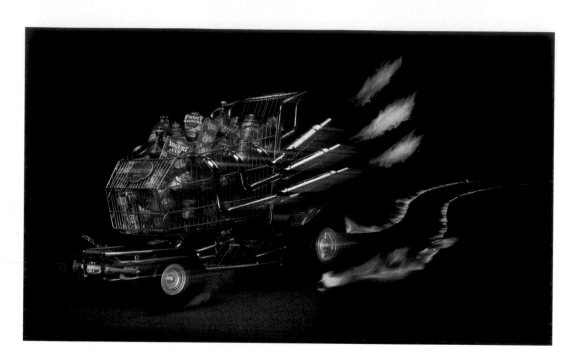

"Shopping Cart." *Larry Keenan was an early adopter of the Amiga system, which is simple in comparison to later developments but which still enables him to make highly effective imagery.*

"Kidswim." *Paul Berger, an art professor at the University of Washington, outputs his digital images to 24″ × 30″ inkjet prints to achieve this unique texture.*

"Disintegration #51." *Eva Sutton's work is the result of many combinations of images that are finally output to conventional film and then transferred to photosensitive cloth.*

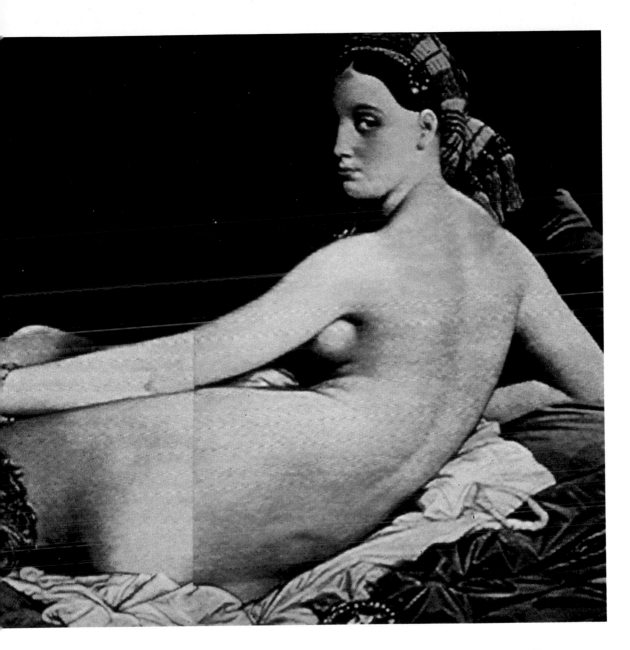

"Perfect World." *Manual is
the "nom de photographie" for
the collaborations of Suzanne
Bloom and Ed Hill, who work
together on a Macintosh.*

Copyright ⓒ 1991 Ron Scott

"Woman's Face in Monitor." *Ron Scott digitally transposed images to place the woman in the monitor.*
"X-rays." *Howard Sochurek specialized in science and medical photography before adopting digital imaging.*
Here he takes X-ray images and manipulates them on his computer.

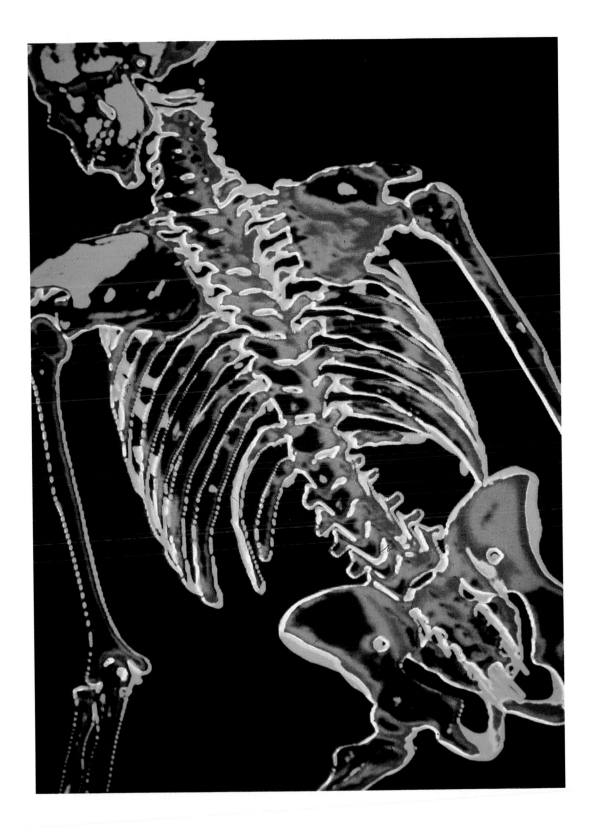

"Nude Woman in Stars." *Ron Scott uses image processing software of his creation to make commercial images.* "Lips Off of Face." *Barry Blackman is a successful New York City–based advertising photographer who has introduced digital image processing to many of his clients.*

"Untitled."
Eric Meola, widely admired for his strong graphic sense and use of multiple exposure, has abandoned his slide copier for a Macintosh.

"Dolobid Man."
David A. Wagner turns a male model into a statue with the help of digital processing. Photography and computer manipulation by David A. Wagner. © by Merck, Sharp and Dohme, Inc.

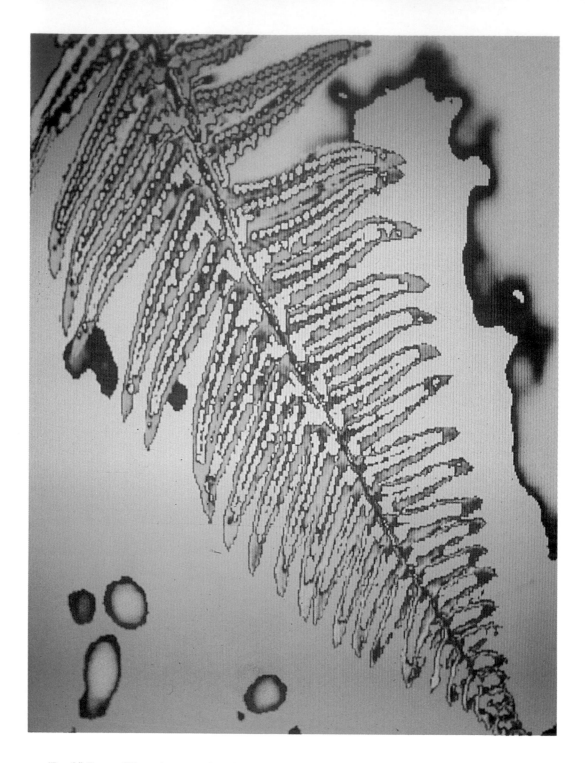

"Leaf." *Penny d'Hamer's art consists of appropriated video images, which she processes on a computer, outputs to a TV, and then photographs off the screen.*

"Cow Punks." *Michael Kienitz has created a humorous contemporary portrait.*

"Patio." *Rob Outwater's work was done with a Macintosh running Adobe Photoshop software.*

"Rocket Launch." *John M. Lund created this work with two different images made in his studio that were combined with image-processing software.*

Part Three
The Possibilities

9.

New Opportunities in Digital Stock, Digital Presentations, and Desktop Publishing

New technologies create new markets, new opportunities and new ways of creative expression for visual artists: witness the invention of motion pictures and television. Digital photography is no exception. What follows are a few of the most obvious opportunities created by the shift from a chemical-based medium to an electronic one. In 10 or 20 years, as the medium matures, today's "opportunities" become commonplace, replaced by other possibilities yet unimaginable.

Digital Stock

Since the early 1980s stock photography has augmented and, in some cases, provided, a primary income for many professional photographers. Digital technologies now offer potentially lucrative new ways of marketing stock images, both for the agency that represents the works of many photographers, and for the individual photographer who wishes to sell his or her own work without sharing the income with an agency.

Computer programs that help organize information about stock images to facilitate their marketing are not new. The first programs appeared not long after the introduction of personal computers in the early 1980s. These stock databases operate much like any alphanumeric database, using text-based "fields" such as Sunset 222, Beach 234, etc., to define and describe photos instead of a file drawer of index cards.

Digital photography, however, offers the ability to go beyond mere cataloging of text/number descriptions to actually catalog and store the image. The benefits are compelling: images can be transmitted and delivered instantly anywhere in the world; and they can be easily duplicated, stored, and marketed in a variety of nonvolatile media, such as CD-ROM and floppy disks.

Over the last 10 years several consumer electronics companies created hardware for the transmission of electronic images, and they have attempted to offer stock images in electronic form to encourage the purchase of their hardware. Generally these attempts failed because the technology was neither sufficiently developed nor widely adopted by the graphic arts community, which is the largest buyer of stock photography. Recently, however, several traditional stock agencies have begun to offer some of their pictures in digital form using formats and platforms already established in designer's studios, such as CD-ROMs and the Macintosh.

In 1988 Comstock, one of the largest stock photo agencies in the U.S., introduced a CD-ROM that contained 441 8-bit monochrome images, saved in the TIFF file format for the Macintosh. These deliberately low resolution images could be used in low-quality newspapers or newsletters (which were not Comstock's primary market, however) but would be unsuitable for most other applications. The intent was partially a marketing test for this new delivery medium, but it also allowed the agency to maintain control over its images. Since the quality of the electronic image was useful only for a dummy layout, it forced the potential buyer to contact the agency for the high-quality photographic transparency for reproduction purposes. At this point the usage fees were determined and the rights administered as in the traditional stock-buying procedure.

Other firms began issuing CD-ROMs and soon more sophisticated 32-bit color images on CD-ROM appeared. Some of the offerings now contained copyright-free, unlimited-use images, much to the dismay of the established stock agencies and professional photographers' organizations, like the American Society of Magazine Photographers.

The next technological advancement was to deliver the image as a high-resolution digital file (as a compressed image) via high-speed modem. With the appropriate software (provided by the agency) now the buyer never had to leave the office. The client could use a modem on his or her computer to search the agency's image database containing hundreds of low-resolution images, which could be downloaded to the buyer's computer and used in dummy layouts. Later, when the final layout had been made, the buyer logged on to the database again and downloaded the selected photographs in high-resolution format. These high-resolution image files could be proofed at the site and displayed on the buyer's computer screens but they never needed to be turned into photographic film again. When the layout was finished, a copy of the digital image file was sent to the printer for conversion into press materials.

The currently favored operating model for selling digital stock, created by Comstock, and likely to be followed by other stock agencies, has been to use digital photography initially as a marketing device that becomes an extension of the stock house's printed catalog. The book provides the selections that inspire the call to the agency. If the client has the necessary computer equipment in place, the stock house sets up an account for electronic transfer of images and provides the necessary software, usually for a small fee. Once a special coded account has been established, all phases of the stock business—research, image transfer, and final selection—are tracked by the agency. This procedure is favored by the agencies since it allows them to maintain control of the images at all times and, thus, protect the images' value.

Much of the digital technology now used by stock houses is also available to individual photographers. Off-the-shelf products make it possible for photographers with limited resources to set up systems that will allow them to send a digital image to a client, provided, of course, that the client is equipped with a modem and a compatible computer. The current limits of the transmission medium (i.e., copper wire versus optical fiber cable) and compression technology, however, do not make it practical for amateurs or the independent professional to send large, high-resolution images this way. Presently, digital transmission is being done with low-resolution images that are useful only for proofing or dummying up layouts. (As discussed previously, photojournalists working for large news organizations, where deadline pressures and newspaper-grade reproduction are factors, are using many of these same technologies to get digital images into print.)

As the technology becomes more sophisticated and its costs decline, it is conceivable that photographers will not need stock agencies with their voluminous files, accountants, and researchers at all. In the same way that answering machines and voice-mail systems have replaced receptionists and secretaries, photographers will some day be able to install an automated image database system that contains all their photographs. Potential clients will be able to phone in, do their research on-line, and order an image—all without the intervention of the photographer. Even the billing will be done and sent by electronic mail. The key to this will be image-archiving software that eliminates all the tedious sorting of conventional photographic images.

To help photographers catalog images there exist a number of database software products that handle both text and images, thereby removing much of the drudgery of filing photographs. Photographs are turned into small digital files, indexed, and stored—not in a big steel cabinet—but on a magnetic or optical disk that you can hold in one hand. Such a digital catalog might work like this: in addition to having a system based on a numerical or assignment-based system, which the user looks up by the correct number or title, the relational database also allows the researcher to request an image by certain word descriptions or facts represented by each photograph in the archive. These descriptors are attached to the digital image file (much like a caption) when the image is entered into the database. Some programs also provide for several lines of text to be entered as traditional captions.

For example, in addition to a filing number, Joe Rosenthal's famous image of U.S. Marines raising the flag on Iwo Jima might be programmed to be filed under any of the following facts relating to the image: "war," "combat," "Marines," "1945," or "Joe Rosenthal." But the image is also symbolic of "patriotism," "valor," and "heroism," subjective words that can also be used to describe the image.

To search the image database, the user types in the appropriate descriptors and a series of "thumbnail" images of limited resolution soon appear on the screen. They are flashed across the screen and line up in a row much like slides on a light table or assembled in a plastic sleeve. At another command, the thumbnails are replaced by a full-screen 24-bit image of the selects. These images can then be printed out, transferred to a disk and sent by courier, or sent over a phone line via high-speed modem.

While these new ways of bringing images to market will be a boon to many photographers, others will be adversely affected. As images become more accessible via the new technology, prices of individual images will surely drop. It's simply a matter of supply and demand. Additionally, the competition between hardware and software companies will in all likelihood force them to provide low-cost, unlimited-use images with their products as purchasing incentives to consumers. Established photographers, accustomed to large fees for one-time use of their images, will vigorously oppose the sale of photographs for these purposes. However, many younger photographers will undoubtedly see this as an opportunity to enter the field and will sell their images to this emerging market. It is expected that new compensation programs will be worked out for these uses. Copyright collectives, modeled after the music industry's ASCAP or BMI collectives, are one option that would be created to collect fees for this kind of sales. In any case, the ability to market and deliver digital stock is clearly a priority for any photographer wishing to remain competitive.

Portfolios on Disk

Many of the techniques used to create digital stock can be used to create stunning electronic portfolios of a photographer's work. In response to our request for images for this book's digital gallery, several photographers sent their work on disks. (They also wisely included transparencies and tear sheets in the event that there wasn't a compatible computer system on which to view their work.) David Brunn (see Chapter 11) sent a disk that contained a note about himself, his resume, and several digitized photographs, both color and black-and-white. He used a software program from Silicon Forest that created a kind of digital portfolio of the pictures on the monitor. One could browse through the pictures singly, or click on a self-running option that presented them slowly one after another like a slide show.

It is reasonable to assume that when the computer becomes as ubiquitous and necessary as a light table to a picture buyer, then photographers will ship around disks rather than lugging heavy and expensive boxes of laminated prints and tear sheets.

Studio Softproofing

One of the major uses of Polaroid film in commercial photography is to create a "proof" of a lighting situation, or as a check of the composition of a set up. Since the paper Polaroid print is tangible, the computer literate might call it a hardcopy, or a hard proof image. If the image were electronic and existed only on a TV screen or on a floppy disk, it might be called a soft proof. And so it is.

Softproofing is a term that sprang up around some of the earliest uses of electronic still imaging in commercial photography. Essentially, it is an image that exists only in electronic form, such as on a TV screen, that largely exists to confirm the composition of the image, not its quality. It requires some sort of electronic input device—a still video camera, a special electronic back fitted for traditional camera, or a scanner. The resulting shot or scan is instantly seen on a monitor. The monitor may be on the set, in another room, or in another city. Electronic images can be sent via coaxial cable or by telephone around the corner or around the world. Softproofing allows a client to see the work he is paying for as it is being made and to react accordingly. It is a helpful technique to some commercial photographers and their clients alike. It allows the collaboration necessary on some complex photographic shoots yet eliminates the need for the client to leave the office.

Service Bureaus

As we have seen, service bureaus provide individual photographers access to the kind of sophisticated equipment required to produce high-end digital results. As more individuals enter the world of digital photography, the number of service bureaus will increase. This means an opportunity for those who understand the photography business and want to be part of the digital revolution.

It is not uncommon for photographers to migrate to the vendor side of the photography business by selling equipment or opening custom labs. The service bureau is the custom lab of the future and some entrepreneurs may want to consider it as a career. Starting up a service bureau will require investment capital of several hundred thousand dollars to equip the facility with high-end scanners and printers, however. The existing photo labs, especially those that cater to the advertising and design sectors of commercial photography, are logical candidates to provide this service. Getting involved with such an operation as an employee or as an investor is a way to gain entry with less financial risk.

Individual photographers who invest in hardware and software on a smaller scale can also perform certain services, such as scanning and retouching, augmenting their income much like a photographer with a basement darkroom who churns out custom prints on a small scale. Many successful photographers started their careers that way and it's reasonable to assume that enterprising young digital photographers can follow the same path.

Desktop Publishing

Since digital photographs can be directly imported into desktop publishing applications, photographers with writing, editing, and designing skills now have an opportunity for creating their own promotional brochures, portfolios, and even photography books. Those who are able to master these disciplines may soon find themselves becoming publishers or, at the very least, gaining control of and making creative decisions about the application and use of their images. One area of the image-making process that photographers had left to others is now returning to the creator of the image: retouching.

Before desktop technology, nearly all retouching in commercial photography was performed by outside specialists or on high-end prepress systems by the printer. The new desktop technology gives photographers a chance to assert creative control by putting the finishing touches on an image. The software can be used for more than removing a blemish or correcting a sky, however. The cut, paste, and blend tools in image-processing software allow photographers to create new images from parts of many others and expand the photographer's role to that of an illustrator, as well.

Authoring Custom Software

Some opportunities, such as authoring custom software, may not be so obvious. Software is a critical component in every digital photographic system. Yet many of the software engineers who create the software that controls the electronic cameras, scanners, and image-enhancement programs know very little about photography. There is an opportunity waiting for the photographer who takes time, learns software programming, and applies these new skills to solving old problems that have plagued photographers, or to seek new and better ways of doing things. Photographers like Ron Scott, whose QFX program is a commercial success, have shown that not only is this possible, but lucrative. (Scott's digital career is featured in Chapter 11.)

10.

Interactive Multimedia

Up until this point we've seen how new technologies can enhance photography and improve traditional photographic tasks. In most cases the end result is a photograph that looks like or is compared with a traditional photograph.

Interactive multimedia, however, uses photographs in a radically different way. For some photographers this will result in a new medium of creative expression. For others, however, it represents a new market for their work.

Interactive multimedia combines photographs, text, sound, video, and even animation to entertain, educate, or inform. Unlike film, video, or multimedia slide shows, interactive media is proactive. Instead of being "fed" images, viewers select their own path through the material using a mouse or infrared remote control. Some multimedia programs also contain a "play" sequence (sometimes called "couch potato mode") whereby the program takes the viewer down a predetermined path of pictures, textblocks, and audio.

Experiencing Multimedia

As an example, imagine that your favorite magazine, book, or newspaper is is front of you. In this case, though, since we are talking about an electronic medium, you will be viewing it on the screen of your home computer, or perhaps your TV set.

There is an article about the Middle East, complete with photographs, graphs and text that interests you. There is only one photograph but, because this is interactive multimedia, when you point to the image with the computer's cursor or control, a slide show begins on the screen. Satisfied, you touch the screen again and the "front page" returns.

This time, as you read the first paragraph, a fact in a sentence intrigues you. You want to know more. Selecting the phrase with the cursor, you hear a voice that relates more information. If you want to remember what is being said, switching on another control button on the screen will bring up a window in which the spoken text scrolls by. You stop it, puzzled by an Arabic word. By pointing to the unknown word, you cause a dictionary definition to appear with the correct pronunciation read by a native Arabic speaker.

From the initial curiosity about a front-page picture and its supporting text, readers have made their own path through several layers of information. In moving beyond what they thought they were originally interested in, users have attained a deeper, richer, more informative experience. Although we are describing a way of using interactive media for news, this format can be used for entertainment and education as well.

Multimedia Today

In the early days, to show or view interactive work required equipment costing well over $5,000. In recent years, however, low-cost players, starting with the first device introduced by Commodore in 1990 for $850, which hook up to TV sets, have become available, and interactive multimedia is attempting to become as pervasive and popular as film or television.

What is deterring multimedia's widespread acceptance is the fact that, at this writing, there is still no single standard or platform for either the software or hardware. CD-I, CD-TV, CD-ROM, CD-ROM-XA, and MPC are just a few of the multimedia formats on the market. It is likely that several formats will prevail for a while until the market determines which has the most desirable features and competitive price.

Personal computers are often used to produce multimedia software,

One of the first multimedia devices for the consumer market was the Philips CD-1 player, which was connected to the home TV. All still and moving images, sound, and the necessary software is contained on the disk. The hand-held remote control allowed the user to interact with the programming by moving a cursor on the screen to indicate commands that affected the programming. The Philips CD-1 also plays Photo CDs.

The Photo CD is a special adaptation of CD technology whereby a photofinisher transfers film images to a disk using a proprietary scanning and disk-writing system from Kodak. Up to 100 high-resolution images are stored on the CD and displayed on the home TV via the Photo CD player (which also doubles as an audio CD player). (Courtesy of Kodak)

which has important implications for photographers who wish to create their own interactive multimedia shows. At its simplest level multimedia can be produced on the desktop with a total equipment expenditure starting at less than $7,000. Ambitious photographers who take the time to learn the necessary skills and techniques can produce compelling work with about the same effort that used to go into producing a basic slide show.

Even though an individual photographer may not be interested in producing interactive multimedia, he or she may be in a position to make it an important component of his or her business. Many photographers have years of stock imagery that producers of multimedia will find useful. Although sales of individual images may not bring huge sums to an individual photographer, the requirements of the medium are such that producers often buy tens or hundreds of images. The final sale may be substantial. Photographers are also being hired to produce original multimedia material and several days or weeks are often budgeted.

Since video can also be a component of interactive media, one may ask, Why should an interactive multimedia producer use still images rather than motion video? Simple economics: it takes a lot of computer memory to store moving images—up to 30 are needed to make up one second on the screen—and computer memory is expensive. Also, the microprocessors required for full-motion video are more powerful and sophisticated than those found in the average PC. Therefore it is much more economical to incorporate still photos than even the simplest video or film images.

In the future, these conditions may change, but the fact will always remain that there is something unique about sequenced still images. The technique has its place even on a screen where one expects continual motion. The classic French movie "La Jetée," produced in the early 1960s entirely with stills, and Ken Burns's much praised "The Civil War" TV series speak eloquently to this fact.

In the following pages are several examples of interactive multimedia. Some of the examples were produced by photographers, others were produced using the works of many photographers. Some were done on the Macintosh platform, while others were done on the PC; some were done on a platform that combines a special playback device with a common home television.

Graham Nash's "Interactive Gallery"

In the mid 1960s British rocker Graham Nash was best known for his music. In the '70s he started making photographs and in the '80s he was collecting them. By the 1990s Nash had brought these interests together in a multimedia program. In collaboration with Rand Wetherwax, his studio manager, Nash has produced the "Interactive Gallery." This is the first step toward what Nash calls the "virtual gallery," where viewers, wearing sophisticated electronic goggles, participate in the artistic process. The idea for Interactive Gallery was born partially because Nash doesn't like captions on gallery walls. However, he admits, after viewing a print, he's as curious as the next person about circumstances surrounding the photograph.

Wetherwax used Director software to create Interactive Gallery, which has as its centerpiece a computer with a 19-inch monitor in the middle of a gallery room, surrounded by huge photographs on the walls. The computer displays 14 images from the show. A viewer, attracted to Nash's image of the singer Joni Mitchell peering though a magnifying glass, moves the cursor to the screen image. The screen immediately dissolves to one where Mitchell is alone, filling the entire screen. There is a small burst of light, in the shape of a heart, on her breast. Click on it with the cursor and it pulses.

Adjacent to Mitchell's image is a caption that describes where and when the image was made. There are several other options. If one wants to hear Nash talking about the photograph, one clicks on a sound icon. If one wants to hear music associated with the image, another click and full digital sound pours out of adjacent speakers. The Gallery is also able to run as an electronic slide show (a couch potato version) that runs continuously.

"Desert Storm" from the Editors of *Time*

The 1991 war between the United States and Iraq has been called a high-tech war, full of sophisticated tanks, aircraft, and smart bombs fitted with cameras that transmitted vivid images of the target instantly back to central control stations. It is also the first event to be packaged and brought to market in the revolutionary new format of CD-ROM.

The editors of *Time* had been preparing a lengthy interactive project on the collapse of communism when a real-time news event gave them an opportunity to experiment with a futuristic version of the newsmagazine. As the deadline approached for the start of operation Desert Storm, *Time*'s editors in New York, and their Time-Warner affiliate Warner New Media (WNM), in Burbank, California, made preparation to create a newsmagazine on disk. When the fighting broke out, every report, audiotaped interview, map, chart, and relevant photograph was duplicated and sent to WNM, where computer programmers, editors, and graphic designers began fashioning an interactive library of the eightweek event. Six weeks after the war ended, "Desert Storm" was pressed, packaged, and ready for distribution, a record time for the fledgling medium. Although only 15,000 copies were pressed, it was a sellout, if only because of its novelty.

"Desert Storm" was designed to run on a Macintosh Plus or newer machine with at least 1 megabyte of RAM. It requires a CD-ROM player and the disc retails for $39.95.

SoftAd

SoftAd is an advertising agency dedicated to interactive media. Instead of creating their clients' messages in the form of posters, magazine advertisements, or television commercials, SoftAd produces commercial messages that are to be displayed on computer media.

Digitized photography is often used in their presentations, and the photos are obtained from a variety of sources; some are provided by the client, others the agency commissions or generates in house. The photos are digitized using a 3-chip RGB video camera and captured through an 8-bit digital capture board. These image files are then converted from 8-bit 256-color files into the appropriate mode, usually 4-bit, 16 colors, using a random dithering interpolation. SoftAd presentations are usually done in the lower ends of resolution, enabling the disk to be played on the largest number of computers. The photos are often touched up with image-processing programs to maximize their display quality.

SoftAd customers include such major companies as IBM, HewlettPackard, Apple, and Volvo. One of their more successful interactive discs was for Ford Motor Company, which contained all the buying information for its vehicles in that model year, along with pictures of the vehicles, an interactive order form that allowed the user to choose various options, a driving quiz, and even a road racing game. A testament to the power of interactive media is that 250,000 people received the disk and actually paid $6 to get what was essentially an advertisement.

Philips CD-I

At the end of 1991 Philips, the Netherlands-based consumer electronics giant, introduced one of the the first interactive devices for the consumer electronics market. Using the CD-I format that they helped define, Philips's "Imagination Machine" came with three discs and a library of 24 others from which the user could choose. The programs ranged from "Treasures of the Smithsonian" to "A Visit to Sesame Street." The new medium turned out to be not only a showcase for photography, but also an ideal way to teach photography. One CD-I disc that Philips released was *Time-Life Photography*, based on the best-selling instructional series from Time-Life Books. The disc contained over 100 hours of instructional material, five hours of audio, 1,000 images, and 25 interactive workshops.

One of the interactive workshops demonstrated the visual effects that can be created shooting motion at various shutter speeds. A full-motion scene of a man in a rowing scull passes across the screen. The user is asked to choose from a variety of shutter speeds and then the action scene is repeated. At any moment in the sequence the user can "shoot" the picture and instantly the picture is frozen at the selected shutter speed so the user can evaluate his results. The exercise can be repeated at other speeds for comparison. The often difficult-to-grasp concept of shutter speed as a creative tool becomes immediately apparent with the instant feedback that interactive media provides.

Time-Life Photography is a popular and innovative program for photography lovers. (Courtesy of Philips)

Multimedia Terms

In an ideal multimedia world, all media—sound, text, images and graphics—would be in digital form. Today much of that media is stored in analog form, however, such as on cassettes, books, 35mm slides, and videotape. These media exist in different forms and to run in a multimedia program they must be integrated in

(continued)

(continued)

some fashion and operated by a computer, which is used as a controller.

Since the invention of the compact disc, electronics engineers have experimented with different ways of encoding digital information. It was found that while sound could be put down in one manner (as in the CDs that contain recorded music) when they wanted to add images to the disc another format performed better. The result was that in the intervening decade a variety of formats for digital information evolved as research scientists discovered new uses of recording digital information.

Until there is a single, inexpensive operating platform for multimedia, the nomenclature will remain cluttered with acronyms. Nonetheless, each platform has characteristics that make it advantageous for certain specific purposes and these formats are likely to be with us in one form or another for some time. Here are some important multimedia terms.

CD-ROM. This stands for Compact Disc, Read-Only Memory. A silvery platter 120mm in diameter, it is the same size as the common audio CD. The most common CD-ROM stores 660 megabytes of unformatted digital data, the equivalent of 825 800K floppy disks. Unlike floppies, however, CD-ROM discs can't be overwritten, which makes them ideal for safely storing data without fear of erasure or of being corrupted during a procedure.

CD-ROMs can cost as little as $2 each to manufacture. The pressing of a CD-ROM is similar to an audio CD, and the difference lies in the way the data is encoded. At a technology conference held in the mountains of Nevada some years ago, a committee met to determine a standard for encoding digital data on CD-ROM. In memory of that conference locale the standard was initially called High Sierra, but it has since become formalized and is more properly called ISO 9660.

In subsequent years, as new technology allowed other media to become digitized, new standards were developed to accom-

(continued)

(continued)

modate them. For example, CD-ROM-XA is an extension of CD-ROM but with better sound qualities.

CD-G is an adaptation of the CD audio disc, but with extended graphic capabilities. This format was developed with an inexpensive consumer electronic device in mind that would allow the user to listen to music while simultaneously seeing the lyrics appear on a TV set along with some low-level graphics.

It is unlikely that the computer market will focus on one CD format in the near future. Each has different capabilities and associated costs so it is likely that they will serve different markets for some time.

Video Laser Discs. These discs hold analog information on a 13-inch format. A laser disc has a capacity of 108,000 frames of video or of still images (54,000 on each side). Originally introduced as a medium for playing movies on TV, it never gained enough consumer acceptance to overtake the videotape cassette in the U.S. It has proven popular for educators, however, and when linked to a computer with multimedia software, it has shown itself to be an effective reservoir for video in multimedia. The laser disc player, when attached to a computer, makes for an expensive and bulky multimedia system, however. Since video images are analog, the laser disc is considered a transitional methodology in multimedia.

Video Laser Disc Players. Not all players of laser discs are alike. A professional version is needed to play multimedia. It transmits a signal with CLV, constant linear velocity, and has a serial port for connection to the computer for control.

HDTV or high-definition television. This standard has more than double the resolution of today's television and an aspect ratio (height and width) that is closer to the ratio of a 70mm motion picture frame. The system is being promoted by the Japanese television industry, while Europe has developed its own HD standard, which is incompatible with Japan's. America, however,

(continued)

(continued)

is resisting adopting one of these new TV standards (neither of which can receive the existing TV signals) in hope that a completely digital system will be introduced that will enable the computer and TV to become one unit, a device that pundits call the "smart TV."

Fiber Optics. Fiber optics are literally a bundle of spun glass fibers. Fiber optic cable transmits data thousands of times faster than conventional sheathed copper cable. The use of fiber optics allows digital color images to be sent in milliseconds rather than minutes. Digital video breaks down a single second of motion into 30 color files that have to be received, processed and shown on the computer's monitor instantly. Fiber optic cable is the best, most efficient carrier of color digital image files.

Visionaries see homes of the future equipped with telecomputers (smart televisions) that are linked to information sources by fiber optics. They foresee them receiving interactive multimedia programming at the phenomenal rate of 1 trillion bits of information per second.

Hypertext. Hypertext was applied to computer experiments in the 1960s in which words and ideas were compiled like a relational database. When activated, hypertext makes surprising associations that inspire unusual nonsequential thinking and writing. **Hypermedia** is an extension of the hypertext idea, which incorporates other media, such as photography, graphics, and sound along with the text. **HyperCard** is an Apple software product, bundled free with the purchase of Macintosh products, which allows users to create a form of interactive multimedia.

11.

Digital
Pioneers

If you frequent a camera store that numbers among its clientele skilled amateurs and local pros, you are apt to overhear conversations about "the good old days" of photography, of times before auto exposure and even of 35mm SLRs. It was a period when the technology was balky; when luck and perseverance played as big a part as talent and drive. Some day soon you'll hear that same conversation about digital photography. Photographers this time will be talking about the early 1980s when the equipment was clumsy, costly, and wholly unpredictable.

Who are the digital pioneers? Some are primarily artists who saw digital photography as new medium of visual expression. Others are gadget lovers who bought anything that was made of metal and wire. Some saw a business opportunity, but too often their enthusiasm for the technology blinded them to the economic realities. They earned little or no money for their investment. Others are academics who live for the process of acquiring knowledge and sharing it with the community.

Pioneers must quickly learn to pool their knowledge or risk being left behind. Due to the far-reaching consequences of digital imaging, the way it reached across academic, technical and commercial disciplines, it has brought together diverse groups of people such as software programmers, electronics engineers, photographers, printers, graphic designers and picture editors. All have skills that they brought to this new medium and their talents have, in turn, shaped it.

The five photographers presented here were chosen not just because they were among the medium's earliest practitioners but also because they represent the divergent backgrounds and outlooks that one can find in a field still in its infancy. Each has had different reasons for moving into electronic imaging, taken different paths, used different tools, and achieved quite different results. What they have in common is not just that their images are based on electronics but that their motivation is based on trying to see something in a new way. This is the motivation of most photographers, regardless of the choice of their equipment.

Ron Scott, commercial photographer/software developer

Ron Scott grew up in Fort Worth, Texas, where his father was an inventor; his mother an actress. Scott remembers being surrounded by an inspiring mix of science and art. Shortly after graduating from Tulane University in New Orleans, with a degree in physics, Scott started his own photography business in 1972. He traveled the country shooting annual reports, was written up in *Communication Arts* magazine, and created dozens of memorable cover photographs for *Texas Monthly*.

In the early 1980s Scott bought a studio in Houston and soon became intrigued by the possibilities of computer graphics. He began a search for an appropriate platform and ended up investing $25,000 in a system that included an IBM PC XT with a meager 640K of RAM, a 20-megabyte hard drive, a 1-megabyte frame buffer, a monitor, and software.

He now laughs at the high cost and low-level results of his first system, but admits that it forced him to learn basic programming and the theories of solid modeling. (Modeling is much like making sculpture with a wire mesh framework. A modeling program is one in which you draw the mesh and then ask the computer to cover it with a smooth skin.) One of his early creations—a brilliant green cactus—was used to promote a well-attended graphics show (SIGGRAPH), where he got his first serious attention as a computer artist.

When the TrueVision TARGA board was announced in 1985, Scott could finally digitize his own photographs and work on them in the computer. His programming skills enabled him to create special effects filters, which he eventually marketed as a software program called QFX.

Around this time (1986–87), while Scott was developing his programming skills, the economy in Houston went into a decline and Scott watched his traditional photography business wither away. His QFX package, however, was developing a strong following, so he turned his attention toward its improvement and then to marketing the program.

Scott is generous with his advice to photographers wanting to get into digital photography but cautions, "It's fun, but if you aren't careful you'll spend all your time retouching and not taking pictures. You can't charge a thousand a day for retouching."

Having the technology on hand that can change any photograph—presumably for the better—can change the way a photographer works. "Just because the computer can be used to fix images, don't use it as an excuse to become a sloppy photographer," he says. "Use it to create a style that is yours. Painterly effects, blurs, whatever. Remember, it is the style that you are selling to art directors, not the fact that it was done on a computer."

Margaret d'Hamer, educator, artist

A self-described "gadget freak," d'Hamer has been manipulating her photographs since 1975. Her first electronic images were made from her own silver halide photographs of President John F. Kennedy. She placed them in front of a video camera, processed with a color synthesizer, and then rephotographed the results displayed on the screen.

"It began with a broken color TV set," d'Hamer remembers. She was enthralled with the saturated color and distorted linear patterns that the TV produced. By adjusting the set's controls she altered the color even more to make abstract designs. Through a "use grant" given by the National Center for Experiments in Color Television, she was given access to more sophisticated equipment and today, at the University of California, Berkeley, where she is a professor of visual studies, she continues her teaching and explorations using Silicon Graphics workstations.

In 1983 d'Hamer became interested in computer graphics. "The ads were quite deceptive," she says, "promising a world with images that often were created by special effects photographers using conventional methods, rather than having been rendered on the respective computer systems."

She took out a loan to purchase an IBM-compatible computer and all the necessary hardware to digitize and display color images, including Easel (now called Lumena), a software program that enables the user to paint color on electronic images.

"My approach is always experimental, " says d'Hamer. "I want to create original graphics and steer away from anything other people do. The early versions of software had very interesting 'bugs' or flaws which, on my computer gave some very odd and interesting graphic effects that I was able to use. Strange as it may seem, these effects can't be easily duplicated now that I have a new, properly working speeded-up motherboard and updated software."

D'Hamer's final hard copy print is created with conventional materials. She photographs her manipulated image directly off a flat monitor with a Hasselblad and prints the images on a glossy grade of Cibachrome paper. She prefers the way the image is rendered on photographic paper rather than by a film recorder. "The monitor has its own individual characteristics which contribute to the look of the final image. It makes what was mechanically perfect much less so, something which, from a philosophical point of view, is more satisfying to me."

Electronic imaging, she admits, has its shortcomings, but it has unique advantages too. "For example," she says, "being able to save the various steps through which a painting proceeds is wonderful. In real painting these steps are always lost as the work develops. Not infrequently the earlier steps are better than the later steps. Such capabilities change one's attitude toward one's work and act to encourage much more experimentation."

David K. Brunn, photographer

David K. Brunn currently lives in Lake Oswego, Oregon, where he works for such clients as Apple Computer and Nike. He is also a teacher at the University of Oregon Continuations Center, and is a former instructor at the Oregon Art Institute. In 1985 Brunn bought his first Macintosh. Using MacVision and Thunderscan, two low-cost scanners available for the Mac, he began to digitize and manipulate his own photographs.

Later he bought a Canon Xapshot, a low-grade amateur-level electronic camera. The design of the handy little Xapshot was such that its images were only suitable for display on the home TV, but Brunn wanted to get control of these images so that he could manipulate them in his computer.

Nearby was a manufacturer of computer board products called Computer Friends, and Brunn convinced them to create a 32-bit video capture board so he could grab the Xapshot's still video images, turn them into digital files and place them in the Mac.

Brunn writes in his master's thesis, "The most important difference between digital photography and conventional photography for me was that I could make images that were made from many objects. This is not new in itself, but what is important is that these objects can be from many sources and have difference scales. In silver photography, the work involved in covering the seams where two images meet or blend is tremendously difficult. With the computer I was able to cover the seams effortlessly. Objects of different scale could be enlarged or shrunk to any size. This instant accessibility to the form of a visual idea was why I used the computer as a tool in my image making.

"The computer's accessibility fed my creative process. I now journey to places that have never been and can never be, except in my imagination."

Lawrence Gartel

Lawrence Gartel was born in 1956, but from all that he has accomplished one would think of him as being much older. He has been involved in computer graphics since the 1970s, and making photographs before that. His manipulated imagery has appeared in *Forbes, Mirabella, Compute* and numerous other national magazines. A book titled *Lawrence M. Gartel: A Cybernetic Romance* was published by Gibbs Smith in 1990. He's also a lecturer at the School of Visual Arts in New York City.

Reviewing some of Gartel's work at an exhibition, the *New York Times* described it as a "love affair between man and machine." Although photography is an important element of Gartel's work, he sees it as just one of several creative instruments that he has used, ranging from crayons to paint. The computer, he feels, is a way of integrating them all.

"This is the art of the 21st century," says Gartel. "To me this is a renaissance—a rebirth of a culture and a unification of science and art."

Gartel isn't particular about any computer platform. He has had access to million dollar installations at such places as the Jet Propulsion Labs in Pasadena, California, but he is equally at ease using a low-cost Amiga.

He was an early user of the Canon still video system, including its FV 540 digitizer, which allowed him to input his images directly into the computer. "You can never take a bad picture,' he says. "I feel free to shoot a lot because a still video disk is so easy to edit and is reusable."

Larry Keenan

There was a time, Larry Keenan remembers, not long after he bought his first computer in 1984, that he canceled a date with a very attractive woman because "I just couldn't get away from the computer," he says grinning, "for anything." Now 47, and married, he has finally managed to modulate his passion for computers. Somewhat.

A 1971 graduate of California College of Arts and Crafts and former high school photography teacher, Keenan's traditional photography has been used by Levi-Strauss, *Omni* magazine, Bank of America, CBS Records, and Apple Computer. His extensive stock collection is handled by The Image Bank. He lives in Oakland and has a studio in San Francisco.

Like many photographers in the San Francisco Bay area, Keenan was introduced to computers in the early 1980s by getting assignments to photograph them. Nearby are the headquarters of such major computer companies as Apple, Hewlett-Packard, and Sun Microsystems, as well as several major microprocessor manufacturers.

Although Keenan was fascinated with computers, they couldn't compare, in his mind, to video games when it came to graphics, speed and color. In 1984 that changed with the introduction of the Commodore Amiga, a reasonably priced, graphically sophisticated computer. Keenan placed an order for one even before seeing it.

He calls his setup a "baby Scitex" (after the hundred-thousand-dollar high-end prepress facility) because he claims that he can do much what a Scitex can do, but without the resolution. Even though the quality is limited, Keenan says a lot of his clients like the highly pixilated computer look. "Without it they don't believe it was done on the computer." His stock agency, The Image Bank, has had considerable success selling his computer-generated photography.

His advice to photographers contemplating making the switch to electronic imaging: "Get some electronics skills immediately. Think of computers as cameras with just a little more electronics. When the passion strikes, go with it. If you don't start learning right now, your kids will be hiring you."

12.

The Impact of Digital Imaging

The effect of the new technology of digital media on the art, craft, and business of photography is far-ranging and will go beyond a migration from film to floppy disks. What the consequences of this shift are, are still being determined. A new paradigm is in the making and at this early stage in its development, there are more questions than there are answers. Many of the questions are, at their core, not all that new but, because they come wrapped in a new nomenclature, they are puzzling to many. What follows is a discussion of some of the issues being debated about the impact of digital photography.

Ethics

As we have learned, the profound ease with which images can be manipulated and their content changed, and the apparent seamlessness of the newly reconstituted image, is an extraordinary boon to the image-making process. Whether it is a personal statement from an artist or a fantastic allegory created for commerce, digital image processing has expanded the possibilities of the medium and empowered photographers with creative resources previously available to only a few.

But with this new freedom, some believe, comes a certain responsibility to use it in a way that does not fundamentally change the way photographs are perceived *as photographs*. The dictum (if it ever really existed) that "a photograph never lies" is itself given the lie when we are confronted with the evidence of some high-end digital image processing where a majestic mountain range can be moved into the background to enhance a product that was photographed in a Manhattan studio.

Those most sensitive to the potential liability of image manipulation are photojournalists—especially newspaper photographers—whose traditional responsibility has been to fairly and accurately employ photography to report the news. They have been in the forefront of the discussion of image integrity since digital image processing first became available to newspaper production departments in the mid-1980s. News photographers operate under severe deadline pressures and judgments about picture selection, size, and placement must be made instinctively and in minutes. Many fear that the image manipulation process will cause random editorial decisions to be made that alter image content for the sake of expediency, composition, or graphic expression, and that in the process, some fundamental information in the image will be lost. Or, it may be that because of the information's absence due to retouching, another meaning is added to the photograph that wasn't relevant to the scene as photographed.

News photographers' concerns reached such proportions that the National Press Photographers Association (NPPA), which consists of some 10,500 photographers, most of whom work for the nation's newspapers, created a standing committee in 1989 to investigate the issue and a year later issued a set of ethical guidelines for their membership. It read, in part:

> "As Journalists, we believe the guiding principle of our profession is accuracy. Therefore, we believe it is wrong to alter the content of a photograph in any way that deceives the public.
>
> "As photojournalists, we have the responsibility to document society and to preserve its images as a matter of historical record. It is clear the emerging electronic technologies provide new challenges to the integrity of photographic images. This technology enables the manipulation of the content of an image in such a way that the change is virtually undetectable. In light of this, we, the National Press Photographers Association, reaffirm the basis of our ethics: accurate representation is the benchmark of our profession.

"We believe photojournalistic guidelines for accuracy currently in use should be the criteria for judging what may be done electronically to a photograph. Altering the editorial content of a photograph in any degree is a breach of the ethical standards recognized by the NPPA."

Later, the organization conceded that some image manipulation is permissible, provided that the fundamental content of the image is not changed. After all, they reasoned, color correction, contrast enhancement, selective burning, and dodging are digital processes that were formerly acceptable in an analog world when the tools were the deft hands of a darkroom technician with a thorough knowledge of the craft of chemical-based imagery.

Other professional organizations, such as the American Society of Magazine Photographers (ASMP), media corporations, and journalism schools have contributed to this debate. Some of the proposals suggest ways of labeling the different types of altered images as being manipulated images, collages, derivative images, or electronically retouched. One proposal, which grew out of ASMP's Electric Picture Roundtable, a year-long, on-line discussion among individuals in the field of digital imaging, proposed that images be labeled in much the same way that software is labeled with version numbers. A version number on a published photograph that had been altered could give the viewer some idea of how radically the image had been changed.

Besides image manipulation, another much-discussed issue among news photographers and editors is the emergence of new possibilities in "picture gathering," a term that describes the process whereby television images are frozen using a frame grabber board and a computer and then are published in a newspaper or magazine. In recent years nearly all the major print media have, in certain instances, grabbed a broadcast TV image and used it to illustrate a news event. Picture gathering is used to meet urgent deadlines that don't even allow for the 20 minutes or so that it might take a photographer on the scene to develop his film and transmit an image to the publication. Critics of picture gathering say that media organizations are opting for picture gathering as a way to reduce personnel costs at the expense of having the unique perspective of a still photographer.

This argument is mitigated somewhat by the fact that many video cameramen and camerawomen are, in fact, still photographers who have moved to another medium. Further, the growing miniaturization of video hardware has enabled a videographer to gradually become untethered from an audio technician and he or she will soon have the mobility and flexibility of a still photographer. The differences between the two perspectives—if there are such—become difficult to distinguish when the persons behind the cameras share the same professional, cultural, and ethical backgrounds. Further, as their tools become less differentiated, as they will, as the resolution of video imagery moves closer to that of today's film imagery, the medium of still video for journalistic purposes will achieve parity with film imagery.

Copyright

Whenever an individual writes a song, book, or play, draws, paints or takes a picture, he or she creates—and therefore owns—what is known as intellectual property. Any photograph, be it in digital or analog form, is protected under copyright laws which, in the United States, date back to 1790. These laws—which have grown in scope as technology creates new ways of expression—are meant to protect the creators of a tangible *expression* of an idea (although not the idea itself) from unauthorized appropriation. Copyright ensures that the creator holds the right to copy, distribute, sell or create derivatives of the original. These rights can be transferred to a second party, but only by the creator himself. (Trademark law, which protects product names, companies or logos is not to be confused with copyright law.)

The latest revision to the copyright laws states that any work created on or after January 1, 1978 will remain with the creator 50 years beyond his or her life. If someone infringes on a copyrighted image by unauthorized publication, duplication, or derivation, he or she is liable to severe penalties.

The fact that digital imaging has made it so easy for another party to duplicate images and combine them with other images in ways that make them unrecognizable to their owners alarms many photographers and their trade organizations. As the technology becomes more prevalent, the number of copyright infringements is expected to grow. The only realistic solution to an anticipated problem would appear to be in education and enforcement. Some of the imaging software and scanner companies have begun to include copyright warnings and advice as part of their product documentation. The publications that computer enthusiasts read frequently advise novice publishers of the consequences of appropriating a photograph or even parts of it.

Enforcing copyright infringement by litigation is only part of the solution. It is believed that some new regulatory and administrative body needs to be created to protect the intellectual property of photographers in a digital age. (In Hollywood, for example, there is a review board, whose job it is to determine if a motion picture is a "derivate" and therefore held to copyright laws or "inspired" and therefore is not.) When photographs can be broken down into minute pixels, moved randomly about and their colors changed at will, it is possible to more easily create derivates of still images than ever before. Just when does a still image composed of parts of another image or images become an original and when is it a derivate? This is a copyright issue that has yet to be addressed.

Another intriguing copyright question is, to what extent will the inevitable copyright litigation impede or halt the progress of technology? Can a scanner manufacturer or image-processing software developer be held liable for copyright infringements done by someone else using its products? Although this may have been partially answered by a Supreme Court ruling holding that VCR manufacturers were not legally responsible for copyright infringements that occurred as a result of home videotaping, similar such cases involving appropriated digital images could limit technological progress.

Pricing

There is one positive aspect of the digital revolution that most commercial photographers and their agents agree on. Digital technology will unleash a huge demand for imagery as more sophisticated publishing mechanisms are being put into the hands of more people for personal and professional use. A. J. Liebling, the much respected press critic of the *New Yorker* in the 1950s, once said, "The power of the press belongs to those who own one." Some 35 years later, desktop publishing brought the power of the press to many more people than Liebling would ever have imagined. By 1990 virtually anyone with a PC could produce a sophisticated typeset document and, in the years thereafter, many experts believe that consumers will want to enhance their documents by including still photographs. But, skeptics ask, will they be willing to pay the kind of rates that photographers have been getting from traditional publishers? It is not likely. Therefore the price of commercial photography will have to be reassessed for this new market.

There are many markets in which the value of a commodity cannot be quantified and photography is one. With the possible exception of journalistic or documentary photographs, in which the value of the image is tied to a specific person, place or time, a photograph acquires its value on the basis of its availability to the right buyer at the right time. Assuming that it meets the generally accepted criteria for technical and graphic excellence, a photograph is worth whatever some buyer is willing to pay for it, at the time that he needs it.

Frequently, accessibility to the photograph is the single determining factor of a photograph's worth. Photograph "A" of a perfect sunset can be comparable to photograph "B" of a sunset. But if photograph "A" is in a stock house where it can be seen and readily accessed, it can earn $5,000 while photograph "B," sitting in a photographer's file drawer, earns nothing. Photograph "A" is really worth no more than photograph "B"; the former is just more accessible than the latter. Digital imaging technology will make this all the more apparent to the picture buyer and the consequences of this will affect commercial photography's pricing structure.

As we learned in Chapter 4, digital databases will make more photographs more accessible, thus creating increased demand, all the while driving down the prices of stock photography. As the stock houses become less of a factor in the market due to price declines, there will be more pressure to sell all rights to images to be distributed on discs. If this happens, photographers will have to abandon the practice of making a huge return on one image for one-time rights while the majority of their images lay dormant in their files. Instead they will have to opt to sell collections of their work as a unit for a significant one-time sale for unlimited use. Or they will have to be prepared to sell their images for one-time use but for considerably less money than before.

If, despite the vociferous objections of professional photographers and their trade organizations, photographers begin selling discs containing all rights to their images, then the market will determine the price. The early attempts at low-resolution images on CD-ROM being offered for all rights started at nearly $500 a disc and declined to $100 in a few years. This is less than the fee for a one-time use of one image in a national magazine when used at a moderate size.

Regardless of the quality of these early images on CD, and how that might have affected their market value, this kind of price structure terrifies and angers most commercial photographers. No stock photographer or stock agency can stay in business at those prices, and photographers rhetorically ask how the seller of all-rights images on disc can maintain a profit margin. Whatever the answer is, it is likely not to please, especially since the cost to manufacture a compact disc is less than two dollars, which suggests that the price of images on CD-ROM can afford to fall even lower.

There have been proposals that the photography industry should create a copyright collective based on the models established by the music industry. There, ASCAP and BMI license music usage to broadcasters, record companies, club owners, shopping malls and other public venues. Through regular surveys and on-site inspection, a pricing model is created that determines each member's share of royalties. Further, the consortium sets guidelines for standard license fees and will act as a clearinghouse for members, if they so desire. The artist would still maintain the copyright, and continue to negotiate other usages of the material, but the many smaller sales that crop up are handled by the collective.

Such a collective would be useful for volume sales of digital images to book publishers, the education market, and private individuals, where the price the user is able to pay is low, but the number of individual sales could be high. Individual photographers could not afford to service those inquiries at that kind of price structure, but a collective could. If this is to happen, however, a significant reeducation of photographers will have to occur. Photographers accustomed to making thousands of dollars on the sale of one image will have to be willing to let a collective sell that image thousands of times but for a few dollars each time.

Environmental Issues

With a photographic system based on electronics, the use of toxic chemicals is significantly reduced. Much has been written on the physical hazards of a chemical-based darkroom. Even with proper ventilation many individuals suffer severe allergic reaction to many of the caustic chemicals that are normally required to process film. The careless disposal of such chemicals can have harmful effects on the environment.

Tough legislation has been passed by state and federal government agencies restricting the dumping of caustic photochemicals into city sewer systems by labs and individual photographers. Expensive recycling equipment is now required to meet these restrictions. New laws have also made producers—not the disposal companies—of toxic waste responsible in perpetuity for damages done by the waste. Heavy fines and jail terms can result from violations. In some parts of the United States, California in particular, water-use restrictions have also been imposed.

Still, electronic technology isn't perfect. It comes burdened with its own kinds of harmful side effects. There has been concern about the electromagnetic field radiation (EMF) emitted by the computer's monitor. This radiation is being investigated as a possible factor in increased cases of some types of cancer and pregnancy disorders. In addition monitors are frequently cited as a source of eye irritation that leads to drowsiness, fatigue, and stress. The frequent use of keyboard, mouse, or other input devices, is the focus of investigations about hand and wrist problems. Called carpal tunnel syndrome and wrist tendinitis and collectively known as repetitive stress syndrome, the affliction is caused when wrist and hand tendons repeatedly perform the same motion thousands of times without rest as in constant word processing.

The manufacture of electronic components is not as clean as the electronics industry would like you to believe. Extremely caustic chemicals are used in the design and manufacture of circuit boards and microprocessors and the disposal of these chemicals is creating problems in some communities, such as those in California's Silicon Valley area south of San Francisco. There, in an area where water is always at a premium, local residents are concerned about pollutants entering the ground water.

Here are some commonly given suggestions for maintaining your health and safety in an age of electronic imaging:

- Keep the monitor away from window light to ensure adequate contrast for screen readability. Use a nonglare screen or add a polarizing filter to your existing one.
- Be sure that proper steps have been taken to protect the computer's user and co-workers from EMF. Check the computer and screen

manufacturers' documentation for the correct working distances to your screen, and, if possible, buy monitors that conform to the most stringent standards available for EMF control.

- Use ergonomically correct furniture to reduce strain from prolonged sitting and inputting. Adjustable chairs, tables, screens, and keyboards enable you to change positions or, if you share a workstation, to adjust the setup to your requirements.

- Take frequent short rest breaks rather than infrequent long ones.

- Support local legislation that provides for the environmentally correct disposal of industrial wastes.

Proprietary Systems

The debate over "open" versus "closed" personal computer systems raged throughout the 1980s and, one would hope, will be put to rest by the end of the 1990s, when it is projected that software applications will be able to skip across platforms and systems with impunity and without concern for compatibility. Until that day, however, the consumer should be aware of the issues surrounding the open- versus closed-system debate, since the consequences greatly affect the individual user.

An open system means that a manufacturer has designed its equipment so that it can be supplemented with equipment provided by another manufacturer. An example is the IBM PC, which went so far as to leave slots open in its computer to encourage other vendors to develop coexisting products.

In this open world, many different talented technology developers work to improve the existing system and, in a sense, create a better computer for the original hardware manufacturer. The computer manufacturer's cooperation gives consumers the benefit of competitive prices and improved products.

Because each add-on product is made by a different company, however, often using different engineering and software approaches, and because they are built in various countries around the world, each with different standards, there is often a serious compatibility problem. You should never assume that all the varying components of an open system will work together, even if they are advertised as doing so. There are just too many variables that have become part of an open system over the years to allow the developer of a new add-on product to say unequivocally that everything in your existing system (computer, peripherals, software) will operate flawlessly with the new product. Any reliable developer will work with its customers to pinpoint incompatibility problems and devise a work-around procedure, however. Open systems also suffer from quality control, largely as a result of the huge diversity of small vendors. Consistency in documentation and support material is also lacking in this environment.

A closed system is one in which a particular manufacturer provides an entire self-contained package. This "turnkey" solution means that there are few compatibility problems, quality is easier to control, and consumers don't have to spend as much time or effort shopping for all the necessary components. Often, closed systems are easier to use because there are fewer variables. When the Apple Macintosh was first introduced it was a closed system, which even required a special tool to open the outer casing. (Subsequent Macintoshes reflect a move toward a more open system.) Closed systems, critics argue, restrict the development of new technologies and they are also generally more expensive, as was the case with the first Macintoshes.

Inherent in a closed system like the Macintosh is a consistent interface that appears across nearly all applications. The closed system software forces all developers to maintain certain standard operating procedures with which the consumer is already familiar. While this may make the software more difficult to create from an engineering standpoint (and therefore more expensive), the familiarity pays off for consumers, who can use the program more quickly and easily than if they had to learn a program that had a unique interface. This fact explains why in the 1980s Macintosh users purchased, on average, more than twice as much software as DOS users. This also explains the huge rush to the Microsoft Windows program in the early 1990s, with which DOS users were finally able to give their computers the advantages of a graphical user interface.

One closed system, in particular, that created a stir within the professional photographic community is the Leafax system. Contained in the Leafax transmitter are a modem, scanner, and specialized software. Associated Press adopted this system for its member newspapers wishing to receive its wire photos digitally. Critics argue that the unit cost is too high, considering the nature of DOS electronics upon which it is based. Leaf Systems, Leafax's manufacturer, argues that because developing a simple solution to transmitting and receiving images was expensive, they are entitled to a return on their investment. Recognizing a good investment when it saw one, the prepress giant Scitex acquired Leaf Systems in 1992.

Computer Security

While this subject may conjure up images of a padlocked terminal or a shrouded screen it really includes everything from preventing simple human error to ensuring against natural disasters to inoculation against electronic viruses.

Any photographer who works without keeping some of the following tips in mind is courting disaster not unlike leaving exposed film in a car's trunk on a hot summer's day:

- Physically secure all equipment, especially computers with built-in hard disks. Be sure that they will not be accidentally bumped, that books won't fall on them, or that a sprinkler system will not drown them. Keep food and drink out of your work area.
- Protect the computer with a dust cover if you are working in a dusty environment. If the temperature in your work area regularly exceeds 90 degrees, consider a cooling fan attachment. Never impede the ventilation openings on the computer's cabinet.
- Back up all crucial data. There are programs that automatically do this at specified times and deposit the latest files on another peripheral. In addition, keep duplicate copies of critical data at a secure location off-site.
- Keep all documentation regarding hardware and software in the same, easily accessible place. Maintain proper documentation of what is installed in your system and update that documentation whenever you make changes. Keep a hard copy (a paper printout) for ready reference.
- Invest in a surge protector, a circuit protection device that thwarts data loss when the power fluctuates or suddenly shuts down. When the power suddenly goes off, however, no surge protector can save data that hasn't been saved. Learn to save data at regular intervals or invest in software that reminds you to do so or does it automatically.
- If you use an on-line data service, protect your password. If you share it with others and the personnel that have authorization to it changes, change the password with the change in personnel.

▪ If your computer disk contains sensitive material and your office is not secure, invest in a hardware or software security system. The former is a lock-and-key device that inserts into the disk drive or attaches to the cables and prevents the computer from being turned on. The latter is software that prevents the system from booting up until you enter your own personal ID code.

▪ Open-plan offices with many computers are vulnerable to thievery. There are devices that bolt or chain the CPU's cabinet to a desk but these devices won't thwart the determined professional.

▪ Have contingency plans for power failure, fire, floods, earthquake, or theft.

Computer viruses are programs that surreptitiously enter your computer system and can wreak havoc or mischief. Viruses are always unwanted, inevitably time-consuming, and potentially dangerous. They enter the computer through contaminated software or can be imported via an on-line data transmission. They are frequently the product of some talented computer programmer with a grudge or a need to show off. Whether it is done as a prank or maliciously, unleashing a computer virus is a crime punishable by severe fines, imprisonment, or both.

By definition, all viruses are infectious, traveling from system to system by network connections or infected floppy disks. As a general rule it's best not to use any program downloaded from a public bulletin board or to use software whose origin is unknown. Most of the major on-line services screen any software that is sent in before posting it for public distribution. But there are hundreds of small, private bulletin boards that may not have the time or resources to perform such procedures.

Any software that does not come in a sealed envelope from the original developer (and some that do!) could be contaminated, and appropriate procedures must be taken before loading it in your system. There are "vaccines" available for curing viruses, many of which are available free, or for a small charge, from local user groups and are available online. When activated, they scrutinize the computer's files for any unusual procedures, identify potential viruses and take action to destroy the virus, if instructed. The consequences, however, are frequent destruction of some data along with the virus.

This possibility makes it more desirable to install a virus protection mechanism that identifies a virus *before* it gets to your hard disk. This kind of software acts as a filter, requiring the user to take action whenever suspicious functions are about to occur. Such software is necessarily more complicated to develop and therefore more costly. But registered users get the added protection of automatically receiving upgraded software whenever a new strain of virus appears for which the antiviral software developer finds a cure.

There is no known method of full protection from computer viruses but vigilance and common sense are the best preventive medicine.

Part Four

The Resources

Glossary

accelerator card: An expansion card that fits inside the computer and contains another microprocessor. It shares the work done by the computer's main microprocessor and speeds up processing time.

algorithm: A mathematical expression that employs formulas to accomplish a specific task. Software engineers design algorithms to establish correct color balance, compress images, etc.

analog: In the field of electronics, it refers to a signal that varies regularly and continuously over its range.

analog-to-digital converter (ADC): A device that converts information from analog to digital form.

anti-aliasing: An algorithm to smooth the appearance of the jagged lines ("jaggies") created by the limited resolution of a graphic display system. Aliasing is caused by insufficient sampling of a digital signal.

application program: A program that performs a specific task, such as word processing, database management, or graphics.

artifact: An unnatural or unintended visual effect observed in the reproduction of an image by the system.

ASCII: Acronym for American Standard Code for Information Interchange (pronounced "ASK-ee"). A standard that assigns a unique binary number to each text character and control character. ASCII is one of the most basic methods for representing text inside a computer and for transferring text between computers or between a computer and a peripheral device. ASCII is a convenient way to transfer files written in one program to a computer running a different program.

aspect ratio: The ratio of the width of an image to its height. For example, broadcast television has a standard aspect ratio of 4:3.

backup: A copy of a disk or of a file on a disk.

bandwidth: The range of frequencies over which a device or communications medium operates. The maximum theoretical rate at which data can be transferred is related to bandwidth.

baud: A unit of data transmission speed. Often, but not always, it is equivalent to *bits per second.*

BBS: Bulletin board system. Usually it is a single computer, accessed by modem, that contains data, messages, documents, etc., that can be retrieved and exchanged by those granted access to the system. (Many are one-person operations run by a volunteer.) Functioning like a post office, it is maintained by an operator to regularly answer queries, initiate new files, clean out dead ones and organize a digital library.

Bezier: A type of curve often used in computer graphic software programs that uses specific control points to set the shape of the curve. The points do not necessarily lie on the curve itself but can function like handles to manipulate that portion of the curve.

binary system: A numerical system that uses only 0 and 1 as digits.

bit: A binary digit in any digital system expressed either as 0 or 1.

bit map: A set of bits that represents the positions and states of a corresponding set of items, such as pixels. Bit-mapped images use only one bit per pixel and therefore take up less storage space than continuous-tone images but, compared with **raster** images, they are more difficult to manipulate and resize.

bus: A path along which information is transmitted electronically within a computer.

byte: A unit of binary information consisting of eight bits.

card: A printed-circuit board containing electronic circuitry, which plugs into one of the computer's expansion slots, allowing the computer to access one or more peripheral devices, or perform a function.

cathode-ray tube (CRT): A custom television monitor used by personal computers. A phosphor coating on the back of the front panel emits light when struck by a focused beam of electrons, producing an image.

CD-ROM: Acronym for compact disc read-only memory; a compact disc 120 mm (4.72 inches) in diameter that can store more than 500 MB of information. The information is designated as read-only memory because a CD drive can read the information but cannot record new information on the disc.

central processing unit (CPU): The processor (often a microprocessor) that performs the actual computations (in machine language) for the computer in which it is installed.

charge-coupled device (CCD): A semiconductor device that produces an electrical output proportional to the amount of light striking each of its elements. A CCD is the principal imaging sensor in electronic cameras, scanners, and video cameras.

circuit board: A board containing embedded circuits and an attached collection of integrated circuits (chips). Sometimes called a printed-circuit board or card.

clip art: Photographs, cartoons, line drawings and graphic illustrations that exist in digital form and are compiled on floppy disks (or CD discs). These images can be copied from the disk and pasted into a document. The term comes from the time when graphic artists, using scissors, clipped pictures out of books designed for this purpose and used them in their designs.

color correction: The process of changing the color balance of an image (or portions of an image) to more closely approach the desired values.

color model: Common models include RGB (using red, green and blue), HLS (hue, lightness and saturation), HSI (hue, saturation and intensity), HSV (hue, saturation and value) and CMYK (cyan, yellow, magenta and "k," which stands for black). The models conform to the way various reproduction media (television, computers, and printing presses) represent color.

color separation: The process of separating a color image in a computer (usually in RGB color space) into a series of single-color images (usually CMYK). Because color printing is done by combining three single-color images and black, color pictures and drawings must first be made into separate images for each of these color inks.

compatible: Applications are normally written to run on specific types of computer operating systems. Those that are able to run on a particular computer system are said to be "compatible" with that computer.

component: In electronics, a video signal in which the luminance and chrominance are sent as separate components.

composite: A composite video signal is one in which the luminance and chrominance information have been combined using one of the video standards: NTSC, PAL, SECAM, etc.

compression: A digital process that allows a data file to be condensed by removing certain discrete data that are not necessary for adequate representation. This allows the file to be more efficiently stored or transmitted. In some instances a file is decompressed and restored.

continuous tone: An image that has shades of gray or color (as opposed to a halftone or bit-map image).

CMYK: A method of representing color based on the standard printing ink colors of cyan, magenta, yellow, and black.

desktop environment: Typical of, but not exclusive to, the Macintosh. It is an operation in which a set of program features attempts to mimic the way people work at an office desk. Commands appear as options in pull-down menus, and material being worked on appears in areas of the screen called windows. The user selects commands or other material by using the mouse or other selector device to move a pointer around on the screen. (The earlier MS-DOS operating system required the use of a series of keyboard instructions to issue commands.)

desktop publishing: Initially, a system that provided the ability to produce "publication-quality" documents on equipment that fit on the top of an office desk. In 1985, when the phrase was coined, the publication was often a newsletter. In the ensuing years, the definition of quality changed as did the sophistication of PCs. Major elements of newspapers and magazines are now produced using desktop publishing (DTP) technology but the peripherals required for publication quality can no longer fit on a desktop, or in a typical office cubicle.

digital: A process that can be represented in a discrete (noncontinuous) form, such as numerical digits or integers.

disc: see CD-ROM.

disk: The medium upon which digital data is recorded and stored. A magnetic material is bonded to a supporting structure similar to audio recording. The disk spins at high speed when placed in the computer's disk drive and the information is recorded in tracks.

dither: A procedure for placing pixels in an area of an image to soften an edge, smooth a jagged line or simulate a shade or tone.

dithering: A technique for alternating the values of adjacent pixels to create the effect of intermediate values. Dithering can give the effect of many shades of gray on a black-and-white display or more colors on a color display to create a richer, better quality image.

DOS: The operating system for IBM and compatible machines. When IBM created its PC it engaged a small software company called Microsoft to write the code for its operating system. Initially called MS-DOS, Microsoft's Disk Operating System drove the IBM PC XT and AT computers. With the IBM PC's success, and later that of clones by other manufacturers, the DOS system came to be the dominant system among PC users.

dot-matrix printer: A printer that forms characters with patterns of dots produced by tiny striker wires.

EGA: Abbreviation for Enhanced Graphics Adaptor, a mid-resolution, limited graphics display system for IBM and IBM-compatible computers. It can adequately represent simple line art, charts and graphs but not photographs.

facsimile (fax) machine: A machine that can scan a page and then transmit an image of the page over telephone lines; a receiving fax machine prints a copy of the original page. The fax machine compresses the data to facilitate transmission time and, as a result, transmits only very low resolution imagery, typically measured at 200 dots per inch.

file: Specific information that has been gathered in one place, named and stored on a disk. In a graphical environment such as the Macintosh the file is represented by a small graphic icon that resembles a file folder and carries its name next to it. In a DOS system a file is given a more cryptic code name by the creator.

filter: A program or "mask" that alters data in accordance with specific criteria, a formula, or an algorithm.

5$\frac{1}{4}$-inch disk: A flexible plastic disk measuring 5$\frac{1}{4}$ inches in diameter and having a thin, flexible paper or plastic jacket. It is more commonly used on older IBM and IBM-compatible computers.

flicker: A visible fluctuation in the brightness of a screen image, often bothersome to viewers over prolonged periods . Flicker typically occurs when the vertical scan rate of the monitor is lower than 50 Hz.

floppy disk: The original disk for the PC was made of flexible plastic with a thin, flexible plastic jacket as well, such as the 5178   178$\frac{1}{4}$-inch disk. These disks could be easily bent, hence the term "floppy." With the introduction of 3$\frac{1}{2}$-inch diskettes, while the disk itself was flexible, its jacket was made of hard plastic. Both kinds, however, are still called floppy disks.

format: The form in which information is organized or presented.

frame: In standard broadcast video, a frame is divided up into two fields, each of which shows every other line in the picture (also called interlaced video). In motion video these fields alternate. When a still image is made with video, the photographer has the choice of selecting a frame (containing two fields and more information) or just one of the alternating fields for a low-resolution, but more compact image.

frame grabber: An electronic device (usually an add-on board) that extracts a single frame image from a video signal.

genlocking: The process of aligning the data rate of a video image with that of a digital device to digitize the image and enter it into computer memory.

gigabyte (GB): A unit of measurement equal to 1,000 megabytes. Typically, a storage device capable of holding a gigabyte or more of information is a mass storage device using digital tape or large magneto-optical platters.

GPI: General Purpose Input, an adapter on the computer that receives whatever clock signal frequency an external peripheral device sends to it, allowing the external device to control the timing and the rate of information in and out of the serial port, rather than the rate being controlled by the computer. Theoretically, this results in faster, safer data transfers, because the external peripheral device does not need to have information about the timing and phase synchronization of the clock cycles that occur in the computer.

grafPort: A shorthand way of referring to a graphics port.

grayscale: A method of displaying black-and-white images in which shades of gray are created by varying the intensity of the screen's pixels, rather than by using a combination of only black and white pixels to produce shading.

hard copy: Information printed on a tangible medium such as paper, as opposed to being stored in software code on disk.

hard disk: A disk made of metal and sealed in a drive or cartridge. A hard disk can store very large amounts of information compared to $3^1/_2$-inch or $5^1/_4$-inch floppy disks.

hardware: The devices that process, display and output computer data.

hertz (Hz): The unit of frequency of vibration or oscillation, defined as the number of *cycles per second*. Named for the physicist Heinrich Hertz.

High Sierra format: The standard adopted by a number of electronics companies to specify a way of organizing information on a CD-ROM. The conference where some of the initial technical proposals were made was held at a resort in the Sierra Nevada mountains. The format is more properly known as ISO 9660.

histogram: The graphical representation of the grayscale in an image. With the horizontal axis representing gray level and the vertical axis representing the number of pixels, a histogram presents an easy-to-read indication of image contrast and brightness dynamic range.

hue: A distinction between colors. Red, blue, green, yellow, etc. are hues. White, black and gray are not considered hues.

inkjet printer: A printer that forms characters or images by squirting tiny drops of ink onto paper.

input: Information transferred into a computer from some external source, such as the keyboard, mouse digitizing pad, a disk drive, or a modem.

input/output (I/O): The process by which information is transferred between the computer's memory and its keyboard or peripheral devices.

interface card: A card that handles the interface (or connection) between the computer and a particular peripheral device, such as a printer, a scanner, a disk drive, or a modem.

jaggies: A colloquial term for the jagged edges formed on diagonal lines of a raster image, typically large type fonts, when displayed on a device of limited resolving power. (see anti-aliasing).

kilobyte (K): A unit of measurement consisting of 1,024 bytes.

laser: An acronym for Light Amplification by Simulated Emission of Radiation. A device that produces an intense source of light that can be focused to a tiny spot.

laser printer: A printer that uses laser light to transfer a page image (sent by a computer) onto an electrostatically charged, light-sensitive drum. A black powder, called toner, adheres to the areas of the drum where the laser has drawn the image. Paper then passes over the drum, picking up the toner, and the toner is heat-fused to the paper as it rolls out of the printer.

local area network (LAN): A group of computers connected for the purpose of sharing resources. The computers on a local area network are typically joined by a single transmission cable and are located within a small area such as a single building or section of a building.

luminance: Brightness, often represented by the letter Y.

machine language: The form in which instructions to a computer are stored in memory for direct execution by the computer's processor.

megabyte (MB): A unit of measurement equal to 1,024 kilobytes, or 1,048,576 bytes.

memory expansion card: A circuit board that adds extra random-access memory (RAM) to your computer.

modem: An abbreviation for Modulator/Demodulator; a peripheral device that links a computer to other computers and information services using the telephone.

mouse: A small hand-operated device that controls the pointer on the screen whose movements correspond to those of the mouse. A rotating ball inside the device moves horizontal and vertical sensors that signal the pointer's direction on the screen. The mouse is used to select operations and give commands.

NTSC: Abbreviation for the National Television Standards Committee, which defines the standard format used for transmitting and receiving broadcast video signals in North America. This standard has also been adopted by Japan and most other countries outside Europe. NTSC defines 525 horizontal lines of resolution and 130,000 elements per picture frame. It is an interlaced display with every other line being refreshed 60 times per second (power line frequency), for a frame refresh rate of 30 lines per second. It requires a monitor bandwidth of 15.75 kHz.

object-oriented: Drawing and layout programs that treat graphics as line and arc segments.

output: The product or representation of information that has been transferred from computer software or memory to some external destination such as the display screen, a printer or a modem.

paint: Graphics programs that treat images as collections of individual dots or picture elements (pixels).

PAL: Abbreviation for Phase Alternation Line, it is the standard format used for transmitting and receiving broadcast video signals in Europe (except for France, French dependencies, and former member nations of the USSR). PAL defines 625 horizontal lines of resolution and 210,000 elements per picture frame. It is an interlaced display with every other line being refreshed 50 times per second (power line frequency), for a frame refresh rate of 25 frames per second. It requires a monitor bandwith of 15.625 kHz.

palette: The collection of colors or shades available to a graphics system or program.

Pantone, Pantone Matching System (PMS): A brand name for a popular method of specifying the colors of printing papers and inks.

parallel interface: An interface in which several bits of information (typically eight bits, or one byte) are transmitted simultaneously over different wires or channels.

peripheral device: A piece of hardware—such as a monitor, scanner, printer, or modem—used in conjunction with a computer and under the computer's control.

pixellation: The occurrence of pixels, large enough to become visible individually, when an image is enlarged. Usually it is the result of insufficient data although it is sometimes used as an effect.

random-access memory (RAM): The part of the computer's memory that stores information temporarily while it is being worked upon.

raster: The pattern of parallel lines making up the image on a video display screen. The image is produced by controlling the brightness of successive points on the individual lines of the raster.

raster image file format (RIFF): A file format for graphics developed by Letraset USA that is an expanded version of the TIFF format used by many scanners. It is used to achieve a higher quality typographic and imaging output.

read-only memory (ROM): Memory that can be read but not easily modified. Information remains in ROM permanently, even when the computer's power is off.

RGB: Abbreviation for red-green-blue; a method of displaying color video by transmitting the three primary colors (dpi). The higher the value, the finer the detail in the image.

RS-232: A common standard for serial data communication interfaces.

SCSI: An acronym for Small Computer System Interface (pronounced "SKUH-zee"). An industry standard interface that provides small computers with high-speed access to peripheral devices such as certain kinds of hard disks, printers, and optical disks.

SECAM: Abbreviation for Système Électronique Couleur Avec Mémoire, it is the standard color format used for transmitting and receiving broadcast video signals in France, French dependencies, and nations formerly part of the USSR. SECAM defines 625 horizontal lines of resolution and 210,000 elements per picture frame. It is an interlaced display with every other line being refreshed 50 times per second (power line frequency), for a frame refresh rate of 25 frames per second. It requires a monitor bandwidth of 15.625 kHz. Although this appears to be identical with the PAL standard, it is not. SECAM also has high-definition standards that allow resolutions up to 819 lines and 440,000 elements.

serial interface: An interface in which information is transmitted sequentially, one bit at a time, over a single wire or channel.

system software: The component of a computer system that supports application programs by managing system resources such as memory and I/O devices.

tagged image file format (TIFF): A file format for graphics developed by Aldus, Adobe and Apple that's particularly suited for representing scanned images and other large bit maps. TIFF is the generally accepted interchange standard for digital images.

touch screen: A uniquely sensitive computer screen that allows the user to select objects and issue commands by touching the screen.

vector: A line segment of a specified size and direction.

video digitizer: A hardware accessory that converts standard analog video signals into digital form for computers.

waveform monitor: An oscilloscope used to display the video waveform.

white balance: A means of adjusting, either manually or automatically, the color balance of still video camera by shooting a white object and adjusting the monitor for a white image.

WYSIWYG: Pronounced "whizzywig," it stands for "What You See Is What You Get," an expression characterizing page processing and typesetting programs or systems that accurately display on the screen the output from a printer.

Bibliography

Books

The Algorithmic Image: Graphic Visions of the Computer Age, by Robert Rivlin. Microsoft Press, 1986. An excellent history of computer graphics.

The Art of Desktop Publishing, by Tony Bove, Cheryl Rhodes, and Wes Thomas. Bantam Computer Books, July 1986.

Basic Digital Photography, by Norman Breslow. Focal Press, 1991. Written primarily with the PC in mind, contains good discussions about TARGA Boards, LUMENA, and TIPS programs.

Beyond Photography, by Gerard J. Holzman. Prentice Hall, 1988. Technical book that details the use of popular software for computers that compile in "C" programs. Contains some evocative images.

Digital Visions, Computers and Art, by Cynthia Goodman. Harry N. Abrams, Inc., and Everson Museum of Art, Syracuse, 1987.

Electronic Cinematography, by Harry Mathias and Richard Patterson. Wadsworth Publishing Company, 1985. Written by filmmakers to introduce video to their cinematographer colleagues.

Electronic Color Separation, by Dr. R. K. Molla. R. K. Printing & Publishing Company, 1988. A well-written book, it focuses on technical problems encountered in high-end scanning. Scanner calibration, color cast correction, tone reproduction and color correction, are just a few of the topics discussed. (Difficult to locate, it can be purchased direct: R. K. Printing & Publishing Company, 120 Fifth Avenue, Montgomery, WV 25136.)

In Our Own Image, The Coming Revolution in Photography, by Fred Ritchin. Aperture Foundation, Inc., 1990.

Interactive Multimedia, edited by Sueann Ambron and Kristina Hooper. Microsoft Press, 1988.

Understanding Electronic Photography, by John J. Larish. TAB Books, 1990. Written by the editor of the newsletter *'Lectronic Photography News*, a good catalog of products and explanation ranging from the early still video cameras to powerful memory storage devices.

The Verbum Book of Scanned Imagery, by Michael Gosney, Linnea Dayton, and Phil Inje Chang. M&T Publishing Inc. Redwood City, California.

Visualization, the Second Computer Revolution, by Richard Mark Friedhoff and William Benzon. Harry N. Abrams, Inc., 1989. This books speaks to a future when the computer will create realistic images without cameras or other input. Beautifully illustrated.

Magazines and Newsletters

Advanced Imaging Published monthly by PTN Publishing Co., 445 Broad Hollow Road, Melville, NY 11747. (516) 845-2700

Amiga World Published monthly by Tech Media, Inc., 80 Elms St., Peterborough, NH 03458. (603) 924-9471

Art & Design News Published bimonthly by Boyd Publishing Co., 5783 Park Plaza Court, POB 501100, Indianapolis, IN 46250. (317) 849-6110

Business Publishing Published monthly by Hitchcock Publishing Co., 191 S. Gary Blvd., Carol Stream, IL 60188. (708) 665-1000

Color Publishing Published quarterly by Penn Well Publishing. One Technology Park Drive, POB 987, Westford, MA 01886. (508) 392-2157

Computer Graphics World Published monthly by Penn Well Publishing. One Technology Park Drive, POB 987, Westford, MA 01886. (508) 692-0700

Computer Pictures Published bimonthly by Montage Publishing Inc., a division of Knowledge Industry Publications, Inc., 701 Westchester Avenue, White Plains, NY 10604. (914) 328-9157

Desktop Communications Published bimonthly by International Desktop Communications Ltd., 530 Fifth Avenue, New York, NY 10036. (212) 768-7666

MacUser Published monthly by Ziff-Davis Publishing Co., a division of Ziff Communications Co., 950 Tower Lane, 18th Floor, Foster City, CA 94404. (415) 378-5600

MacWeek Published weekly by Coastal Associates Publishing, One Park Ave., New York, NY 10016. (609) 461-2100.

Macworld Published monthly by Macworld Communications, Inc., 501 Second Street, San Francisco, CA 94107. (415) 243-0505

Mondo 2000 Published quarterly. P.O. Box 10171, Berkeley, CA 94709. (510) 845-9018

New Media Published monthly. 901 Mariner's Island Blvd., Suite 365, San Mateo, CA 94404. (415) 573-5170

PC World Published monthly by IDG Communications, Inc., 501 Second Street, San Francisco, CA 94107. (415) 243-0500

Photo District News Published monthly except for May and October, when one extra issue is printed per month. 49 East 21st Street, New York, NY 10010 (212) 677-8418

RIT Newsletter Published quarterly. P.O. Box 9887, Rochester, NY 14623

TypeWorld Published twice a month by Penn Well Publishing, One Technology Park Drive, POB 987, Westford, MA 01886 (508) 392-2157.

Verbum Published quarterly By Verbum Inc., P.O. Box 12564, San Diego, CA 92112. (619) 233-9977

Off-the-shelf Software Programs

For the Macintosh. There are at least three color editing programs for the Macintosh, Photoshop, PhotoMac, and ColorStudio, and two very good black-and-white editing programs, ImageStudio and Digital Darkroom.

Photoshop. Photoshop is by far the leading image-processing software package for the Macintosh. It is sold by Adobe, a developer of digital typography software, which has invested considerably in its refinement.

Photoshop is a 24-bit full-color image processor with built-in painting and prepress capacities. It includes free selection, as well as a "magic wand" for making automatic selections. Since it uses virtual memory it will work with any size image even with only two megabytes of RAM. The program comes with a wide range of filters including image sharpening, softening, blur, a soft edge blur, mosaic, and diffusing. Colors can be adjusted in several ways: through brightness controls, contrast, hue, and saturation. A histogram, to map the distribution of contrast throughout the image, is also included.

Adobe Photoshop
Adobe Systems Incorporated
1585 Charleston Road
P.O. Box 7900
Mountain View, CA 94039-7900
(415) 961-4400 or (415) 543-9500

ColorStudio. ColorStudio is another excellent 24-bit image editing processor for the Macintosh. Like Photoshop, it comes with CMYK to RGB conversion and produces Scitex output that can be directly ported over to a high-end prepress system for the highest possible output quality. ColorStudio has sophisticated color mapping tools, which allows easy adjustment of gamma. Paint tools are very flexible, although ColorStudio's interface is not as intuitive as Photoshop's. A 24-bit card is recommended but it will work on an 8-bit card as well.

ColorStudio
Letraset USA
40 Eisenhower Drive
Paramus, NJ 07653
(201) 845-6100

PhotoMac. PhotoMac was introduced in 1988 and was the first 24-bit color image-processing software for the Macintosh. There are two very special features: First is the clever way that PhotoMac works with 24-bit files on a standard Mac II 8-bit board. Second is the use of a virtual memory system that allows for the editing of extremely large images using a standard Mac II equipped with only 2MB of RAM. (The largest image PhotoMac will handle, assuming there is enough available disk space, is 32,000 x 32,000 pixels.)

By using a video board, such as Data Translation's Color Capture frame-grabber board (a 16-bit board), a standard NTSC signal can be sent or received. This means images from video cameras, still video cameras, and VCRs can be placed directly into PhotoMac for editing and exported.

PhotoMac
Data Translation, Inc.
100 Locke Drive
Marlboro, MA 01752
(800) 522-0265 or (508) 481-3700
Requires a Macintosh II (IIx) with at least 2MB RAM, a 40-megabyte hard disk, and the standard Apple 8-bit video card. System 6.0.2 or later. Not copy-protected.

Digital Darkroom. At this writing Digital Darkroom is the most feature-laden of the 8-bit black-and-white editing programs available for the Macintosh. Digital Darkroom's key features include: free 360° rotation, as well as scaling, stretching, slanting, and distorting of grayscale images; a Magic Wand selection tool that selects according to contiguous gray values; AutoTrace, which converts bit-mapped images into vector-oriented images, and an "Advanced Halftone" printing option, which improves details and better gray graduation on halftones produced on laser printers. The main drawback is that the program doesn't use any virtual memory management.

Digital Darkroom
Aldus Consumer Division
9770 Carroll Center Road, Suite J

San Diego, CA 92126
(619) 695-6956
Macintosh Plus, SE, or II
Recommended system 6.0

ImageStudio. This was the first 8-bit monochrome image editing program for the Macintosh. ImageStudio's strength lies in its extensive painting tools and variety of filters. The rubber stamp tool is unique, allowing one to create custommade designs, such as a candy cane or leaf, that can then be stamped anywhere on the photograph. The water drop tool, which blends adjacent grays, is a great retouching tool as is the fingertip tool, which smears grays together. The program is well written and commands execute quickly.

ImageStudio
Letraset USA
40 Eisenhower Drive
Paramus, NJ 07653
(201) 845-6100

For DOS Computers. At this writing there is one full-color image-processing software package for DOS-based PCs, PhotoStyler, and at least four programs that enhance or alter grayscale photographic images, Gray F/X, Picture Publisher, ImagEdit, and Image-In. All of the above software run on a 286 or faster computer using standard VGA monitor or better.

Sophisticated color image processing on a DOS PC requires add-on digital image-processing boards and special software. The best known of these boards are the TARGA and Vista/NuVista, boards from TrueVision (see below).

PhotoStyler. PhotoStyler is the first off-the-shelf product for DOS-based PCs that processes 24-bit color without the need of special digital processing boards and software, such as that offered by TrueVision (see below). PhotoStyler works under Windows 3.0, and it takes advantage of both Window's 24-bit capabilities and its memory management system. (Although PhotoStyler will work with a standard VGA monitor, in order to view 24-bit color on a monitor, a 24-bit display card is needed.) PhotoStyler offers many of the same image-processing features as Photoshop, including a variety of editing and color correcting tools. Color separations are also possible (with adjustments for different types of printing papers). The program accepts all popular file formats as well as the TARGA file format. Since it is marketed by Aldus, it is fully compatible with all Aldus products including Pagemaker.

Requires: 286-, 386-based computer with VGA or better graphic device/ display.

Aldus Corporation
411 First Avenue
Seattle, WA 98104-2871
(206) 628-2320

Gray F/X. Gray F/X is, with a few minor limitations, a good model of how a gray-scale processor should perform. It doesn't require Microsoft Windows and is easy to load. It clearly displays 64 shades of gray so work can be done with accuracy and detail. (It may display up to 256 shades, depending on your hardware configuration.) Unlike Picture Publisher, all tools and controls are on the same screen as the grayscale image. The tools are intuitively accessed and responsive.

Requires: 286-, 386-based computer with a Gray F/X–supported VGA graphic device/display. 640K memory minimum, extended and expanded recommended. 10MB free on hard disk. DOS 3.0 or later.

Xerox Imaging Systems, Inc.
9 Centennial Drive
Peabody, MA 01960
(800) 248-6550
Version: 1.0 comes in 3½- and 5¼-inch disks

Picture Publisher. Picture Publisher has all the tools and options you'll probably ever need. For making selections you have no fewer than six choices: freehand, rectangle, square, circle, ellipse, and automask, which finds and selects edges automatically. To alter and enhance gray values, there are at least six choices from simple brightness/contrast control to posterize to an interactive tone map. There is even a unique "Quartertone" option that helps you isolate and make specific decisions and changes to four tonal values, ranging from highlight to shadow. There are 10 retouching tools: paint, sharpen, smooth, spray, clone, and smear, just to name a few. And finally, eight editing tools from cut to blend to mirror and crop.

Picture Publisher works with Windows. When you open the program and open a file, a dithered version is displayed, along with various menu controls for tools and options. You can't work on the dithered image; you must enter the "editing mode" or "Astral Picture Window" as Picture Publisher calls it. Click on Exchange and you now see an image with all the grays intact and a new set of options and tools.

Requires: PC/XT/AT PS/2 or Compatible. VGA or MCGA graphic card and VGA-compatible monitor. 640K RAM and hard disk. Windows 2.03 or higher. DOS 3.0 or higher.

Micrographics
1303 Arapaho Road
Richton, TX 75081

(214) 234-1769
Version: 2.0 comes with 5¼-inch high density disks (3½-inch available)

ImagEdit. This is the only Windows program that puts a grayscale image and total editing control in one window. (A dithered image is an option.) It also has command keys for just about everything, an easily accessed pull-down menu, and standard icons on the side for various editing functions. In other words, it has all the makings of an excellent program, only a few basic things are missing. There is no freehand selection tool; no despeckle tool (which automatically gets rid of noise often encountered in scanning); no blur or smudge tool (almost essential for detailed work); and no sharpening or soft focus filters.

Requires: 286-, 386-based computer with ImagEdit-supported VGA or better graphic device/display. A minimum of 640K of system memory. Expanded memory recommended. Hard drive with at least 2MB free. Windows 2.0 or higher. DOS 3.3 or higher.

IBM
Old Orchard Road
Armonk, NY 10504
(914) 765-1900
Version: 2.0 comes in 3½- and 5¼-inch disks

Image-In. Image-In is an integrated program for document retrieval and image processing and several add-on modules are available for OCR and image vectorization. It runs under Microsoft Windows and has a full set of paint and image enhancement tools. It reads and saves in nine file formats.

Requires: 286-, 386-based computer with supported VGA graphic device/display. 512K of system memory. Expanded and/or extended memory recommended. Hard drive with several MB of available space. DOS 3.1 or higher. Windows 2.03 or higher.

Version: 1.02 comes in 3½- and 5¼-inch disks

Image-In Incorporated
406 East 79th Street
Minneapolis, MN 55420
(612) 888-3633

TrueVision Products for DOS Computers. The first color-processing product ever developed for personal computers was the TARGA board for the IBM PC. Originally made and marketed by AT&T, it is now sold by TrueVision, a spin-off of AT&T. TrueVision has gone on to develop a higher resolution graphic board called the Vista board (available for both the PC and the Macintosh). TrueVision boards not only contain their own microprocessors but will capture and digitize images from video sources as well. A second monitor is required to utilize their capabilities fully. Special software, as noted below, must also be used.

Painting Programs for TrueVision Boards. *TIPS*, which stands for Truevision Image Processing Software, is a program by Island Graphics designed to be used with a TARGA board. Different versions are needed for each board. It comes bundled with the TARGA 16 and M8 boards. It is a basic paint program, limited by addressable resolution and features.

LUMENA is considered the top-of-the-line paint program for TrueVision boards. It has many more features than TIPS, such as 3-D rendering and graphic capabilities. It also includes limited tone/color correction capabilities.

RIO, or *Resolution Independent Object*, is a graphic package (not really a paint package) that treats objects as vectors instead of bit maps. The program is useful, however, when used with another paint program to combine graphic elements with photos.

QFX and *HiRes QFX*, by Ron Scott, Inc., start where many of the above paint programs leave off. Both are image-processing programs for the Vista and TARGA 16, 24, and 32 boards (as well as for the ARTISTR RealVision TM 16E). The programs include filters for sharpening images, softening images and detecting edges in images. Custom filters can also be created. Glow, Emboss and Shadow functions let one create effects with the same names. Remap makes high contrast and posterization effects; global color edits in the LHS color space mode. QFX uses "alpha composition" for smooth, jaggy-free compositions. There are also image control functions for tonal changes.

Ron Scott, Inc.
1000 Jackson Boulevard
Houston, TX 77006
(713) 529-5868

Norman Breslow's Painting Effects offers programs designed to convert photographs into painting-like imagery. Versions are available for normal and HiRes TARGA-16 images.

Norman Breslow's Painting Effects
12021 Wilshire Boulevard, Suite 290
Los Angeles, CA 90025
(310) 478-6056

For Commodore Amiga. There are several excellent image-editing packages available for the Amiga. Most of the Amiga programs are made specifically either for painting or tone/color correction. At this time there is no single package that adequately does both.

PIXmate, for example, is an imaging program with no painting or retouching tools. However it has a variety of sophisticated tone and color correction tools and a histogram.

Progressive Peripherals & Software
464 Kalamath Street
Denver, CO 80204
(303) 825-4144

Art Department Professional is another program with powerful color/tone correction tools (including gamma control and a histogram). The program also contains a file converter so that IFF (the Amiga file format) can be translated into a variety of other formats, including TIFF.

ASDG Inc.
925 Stewart Street
Madison, WI
(608) 273-6585

Painting/Retouching programs available for the Amiga include *Delux Paint III* and *Delux PhotoLab* (both by Electronic Arts), *Digi-Paint 3* (by NewTek, the same company that offers the Digi-View digitizer), and *Photon Paint* (by Hollyware).

Electronic Arts
1450 Fashion Island Boulevard
San Mateo, CA 94404
(415) 571-7171

Hollyware
13464 Washington Boulevard
Marina Del Rey, CA 90291
(310) 822-9200

NewTek
215 East 8th Street
Topeka, KS 66603
(913) 354-1146

Manufacturers and Developers of Equipment and Software

Adobe Systems Inc.
(Photoshop imaging software)
1585 Charleston Road
P.O. Box 7900
Mountain View, CA 94039
(415) 961-4400
(415) 543-9500

Aldus Corporation
(Digital Darkroom and PhotoStyler imaging software)
411 First Avenue, Suite 200
Seattle, WA 98104
(206) 628-2320

Apple Computer Inc.
(Macintosh computers)
20525 Mariani Avenue
Cupertino, CA 95014
(408) 996-1010

Array Technology
(overhead scanners)
7730 Pardee Lane
Oakland, CA 94621
(510) 633-3000

AST Research Inc.
(flatbed scanners)
10215 Alton Parkway

P.O. Box 19658
Irvine, CA 92713-9658
(800) 727-1278
(714) 727-4141

AXS
(image database systems)
2560 9th Street, Suite 219
Berkeley, CA 94710
(510) 540-5232

Barneyscan Corp.
(film scanners)
P.O. Box 14467
Oakland, CA 94614-2467
(510) 562-2480

Broderbund Software
(multimedia products)
500 Redwood Boulevard
Novato, CA 94948
(415) 382-4400
(415) 382-4700

Canon USA Inc.
(electronic cameras, color photo copiers, still video digitizers)
One Canon Plaza
Lake Success, NY 11042

(516) 488-6700

C-Cubed
(compression devices)
1778 McCarthy Boulevard
Milpitas, CA 95035
(408) 944-6300

Computer Friends Inc.
(video cards, digitizers, image-organizing software)
14250 NW Science Park Drive
Portland, OR 97229
(503) 626-2291

Data Translation
(video capture boards)
100 Locke Drive
Marlboro, MA 01752
(508) 481-3700
(800) 522-0265

DEST Corp.
(flatbed scanners)
1015 East Brokaw Road
San Jose, CA 95131
(408) 436-2700

Dicomed Inc. (formerly Crosfield)
(high-end drum scanners)

11401 Rupp Drive
Burnsville, MN 55337
(612) 895-3000

Eastman Kodak Company
(electronic cameras, flatbed and film scanners, digital color printers, Photo CD systems)
343 State Street
Rochester, NY 14650
(800) 233-1650

Hewlett-Packard
(flatbed scanners and laser printers)
16399 West Bernardo Drive
San Diego, CA 92127
(619) 592-8010

Howtek Inc.
(flatbed scanners and printers)
21 Park Avenue
Hudson, NH 03051
(603) 882-5200

Iris Graphics Inc.
(inkjet printers)
6 Crosby Drive
Bedford, MA 01730
(617) 275-8777

Konica
(electronic cameras)
71 Charles Street
Glen Cove, NY 11542
(516) 674-2500

Lapis Technology
(monitors, video boards)
1100 Marina Village Parkway
Suite 100
Alameda, CA 94501
(510) 748-1600

Letraset USA
(ColorStudio and ImageStudio imaging software)
40 Eisenhower Drive
Paramus, NJ 07653
(201) 845-6100

Light Source
(imaging software)
17 East Sir Francis Drake
Boulevard, Suite 100
Larkspur, CA 94939
(415) 461-8000

Linotype Co.
(digital typesetters)
425 Orser Avenue
Hauppauge, NY 11788
(516) 434-2000

Logitech Inc.
6505 Kaiser Drive
Fremont, CA 94555
(510) 795-8500

Macromedia (formerly MacroMind)
(multimedia software, including "Director Interactive")
600 Townsend Street
San Francisco, CA 94103
(415) 442-0200

Mass Micro Systems
(storage devices)
810 West Maude Avenue
Sunnyvale, CA 94086
(408) 522-1200

Microsoft Corp.
(software)
1 Microsoft Way
Redmond, WA 98052-6393
(206) 882-8080

Microtek Inc.
(flatbed and film scanners)
680 Knox Street
Torrance, CA 90502
(213) 321-2121

Mitsubishi Electronics America Inc.
(flatbed scanners)
5665 Plaza Drive
Cyprus, CA 90630
(714) 220-2500

NeXT
(workstation computers)
900 Chesapeake Drive
Redwood City, CA 94063
(415) 366-0900

Nikon Electronic Imaging
(slide scanners, thermal dye printers, transmission devices)
1300 Walt Whitman Road
Melville, NY 11747
(516) 437-4355

RasterOps Corporation
(monitors, video boards, printers, slide scanners)
2500 Walsh Aveune
Santa Clara, CA 95051
(408) 562-4200

Savitar
(color calibration software)
139 Townsend Street
Suite 203
San Francisco, CA 94117
(415) 243-3030

Scitex American Corp.
(drum scanners)
5120 West Sololeaf Circle
Los Angeles, CA 90056
(213) 292-3600

Sharp Electronics Corp.
(flatbed scanners)
Sharp Plaza
Mahwah, NJ 07430-2135
(800) BE-SHARP (237-4277)
(201) 529-8200

Silicon Graphics
(workstation computers)
P.O. Box 7311
2011 North Shoreline
Boulevard
Mountain View, CA 94043
(415) 960-1980

Sony Corporation
(electronic cameras, printers,

transmission devices)
Sony Drive
Park Ridge, NJ 07656
(201) 930-6576

Storm Technology
(compression boards,
compression software)
1861 Landings Drive
Mountain View, CA 94043
(415) 691-6600

Sun Microsystems Inc.
(workstation computers)
2550 Garcia Avenue
Mountain View, CA 94043
(415) 960-1300

SuperMac Technology
(video boards, monitors)
485 Potrero Avenue
Sunnyvale, CA 94083
(408) 245-2202

Thunderware Inc.
(imaging software, scanners)
21 Orinda Way
Orinda, CA 94563
(415) 254-6581

Truevision Inc.
(video boards, imaging software)
7340 Shadeland Stations
Suite 100
Indianapolis, IN 46256
(800) 858-TRUE (858-8783)

Selected Service Bureaus

(Service Bureaus are listed under "Computers" or "Computer Services" in the Yellow Pages)

Basic Images II
P.O. Box 23563
Oakland, CA 94623-0563
(510) 482-3992

Colorscape Communications
625 2nd Street, Suite 308
San Francisco, CA 94107
(415) 979-0922

Duggal
9 West 20th Street
New York, NY 10011
(212) 242-7000

**Printz Electronic Design
Service**
340 Townsend Street
San Francisco, CA 94107
(415) 543-5673

Ron Scott, Inc.
1000 Jackson Boulevard
Houston, TX 77006
(713) 529-5868

Distributors, Producers, and Displayers of Computer Interactive Media

**Interactive Media
Association (IMA)**
3 Church Circle, Suite 800
Annapolis, MD 21401
(410) 626-1380

Optical Data
30 Technology Drive
Box 4919
Warren, NJ 07059
(908) 668-0022

PF. Magic (formerly
Interactive Productions)
501 2nd Street, Suite 108
San Francisco, CA 94107
(415) 495-0400

**Philips Interactive Media of
America**
11111 Santa Monica
Boulevard, Suite 700
Los Angeles, CA 90025
(310) 444-6600

Tech 2000
(interactive media museum)
800 K Street NW
Washington, DC 20001
(202) 842-0500

Tor Productions
139 Townsend Street
Suite 203
San Francisco, CA 94117
(415) 243-3928

Voyager Company
1351 Pacific Coast Highway
Third Floor
Santa Monica, CA 90401
(310) 451-1383

Warner New Media
3500 Olive Avenue
Burbank, CA 91505
(818) 955-9999

Education/Conferences/
On-line Photographic
Forums

Education

In the last few years, many schools have added digital photography courses to their curriculum. Some schools, such as the Rochester Institute of Technology, have even devoted entire departments toward careers in electronic imaging.

RIT is the first college in the United States that offers a Ph.D. in imaging science. (Major sponsors of the program include Eastman Kodak, Polaroid, Fuji, Xerox Konica, Dai Nippon, and Mitsubishi Paper Mills.) Students seeking admission hail from varying backgrounds that include prepress, video, and photography. The school encourages an interdisciplinary background and often turns down students who don't have it. Graduates are quickly sought by many imaging companies.

Other major schools that are becoming leaders in the use of digital photography include Platt College in San Diego, Ansel Adams Center in San Francisco, Illinois Institute of Technology in Chicago, and, in New York City, The School of Visual Arts, Pratt, and the New York Institute of Technology.

Professional photographic organizations such as the American Society of Magazine Photographers (ASMP), the National Press Photographers Association (NPPA), and Advertising Photographers of America (APA) also provide courses, lectures, and weekend seminars. Photo Expo (organized by Conference Management Corporation and promoted through the Photo District News) also provides digital photography instruction as exhibitions.

NPPA is one of the more active organizations in this area and has sponsored a yearly conference on Digital Photography since 1986. Starting in 1989 they have sponsored a workshop where manufacturers of digital hardware and software bring their state-of-the-art products for some 50 qualified participants to use in a real-world scenario. With the assistance of some of the leading practioners in digital imaging serving as faculty, the attendees actually write, photograph, and design a newspaper, called *The Electronic Times*, which is printed up and distributed.

Private seminars are also available, sometimes sponsored by vendors of various equipment.

One of the best ways of becoming familiar with digital photography, besides taking a course, is by joining a computer users group located in most major cities. User groups are generally oriented toward one type of computer platform. Within the computer groups are subgroups (or SIGs, Special Interest Groups), which are more specifically tailored toward individual topics or disciplines such as database management, publishing, and multimedia.

The electronic bulletin boards (BBS) that are reached via modem exist on various on-line services. They are another convenient way to tap into what is happening in digital photography. They provide up-to-date information about the latest developments in digital imaging and photography in general. Bulletin boards are found on such electronic information services as Compuserve, America Online, GEnie and Prodigy. Most BBS contain not only a wealth of information but are interactive too. Forums exist where specific topics are raised and various members contribute. Most forums are monitored and managed by someone with expertise in that particular area to ensure knowledgeable and reliable responses to inquiries.

Conferences

Macworld (*held twice annually*)
Mitch Hall Association
P.O. Box 4010
Dedham, MA 02026
(617) 361-2001

NPPA Digital Photography Conference (*annual*)
National Press Photographers Association
3200 Croasdaile Drive, Suite 306
Durham, NC 27705
(919) 383-7246

Photo Expo Conference Management Corp.
200 Connecticut Avenue
Norwalk, CT 06856-4990
(203) 852-0500

Seybold (*twice annually*)
29160 Heathercliff Road, Suite 200
Malibu, CA 90265
(800) 777-6650
(310) 457-5850

Siggraph (*annual*)
Conference Management Office
401 North Michigan Avenue
Chicago, IL 60611
(312) 644-6610

On-line Photographic Forums

Compuserve
5000 Arlington Center Boulevard
Columbus, OH 43220
(614) 457-8600

Press Link
One Herald Plaza
Miami, FL 33132
(305) 376-3818

Prodigy Services Co.
445 Hamilton Avenue
White Plains, NY 10601
(800) 745-5409
(914) 962-0310

Index